Donald G. Butler

Teaching Yoga

Pelham Books
London

First published in 1975

Republished with amendments by
Pelham Books Ltd
44 Bedford Square
London WC1B 3DU
1980

ISBN 0 7207 1237 8

Printed in Great Britain by
Hollen Street Press Ltd at
Slough, Berkshire and
bound by Dorstel Press Ltd
at Harlow, Essex

Contents

Acknowledgement
Three people have contributed especially to the making of this book:
Jane Russell, a Yoga student, who posed for the demonstration photographs;
Malcolm McCullough, who took the photographs;
Mrs Joyce Ferguson, who typed the script.
To each of these good friends I am deeply indebted.

1: Introduction

A need, a challenge, a problem and an opportunity

Yoga has never been so popular. It is impossible even to hazard a guess as to the number of men and women, boys and girls – people of all ages, from all walks of life, healthy and ill – who are practising Yoga.

There seem to be several common methods of 'following the subject', 'learning the art' – call it what you will – depending on your approach.

1. A great many people are learning Yoga from books. There are very many on the market. It is possible to learn from books, but there are difficulties, notably in memorising sufficiently to be able to lay the book aside whilst actually being engrossed in the doing of it. It is also not easy to know whether your posture is correct, your breathing technique suited to your own condition, or your failure to attain early success with concentration a sign that Yoga is not for you. Books are best used as an aid to memory in conjunction with a teacher.

2. There must be thousands of housewives and others whose interest has been fired by Yoga on television. Once again, it is not easy to memorise what you see, and it is important to have a book, especially one that is designed to be used with the television programme. But the problems arise again: 'Am I doing what I should? Am I making progress? I wish I could ask a few questions.'

3. Up and down the country Yoga classes are in operation: there are classes in all the large cities and towns. Many country areas have no classes within easy reach. Going to a class is, for most people, the best and most satisfying way of

learning. Once again though, there are problems. Experience has proved beyond doubt that the best size for a Yoga class is fifteen to twenty pupils, and even then, it is helpful if the teacher can have the assistance of one or two experienced demonstrators. But this is universally very far from the case. Enrolments for classes almost always exceed expectations by two or threefold. It is not uncommon for a class to be arranged with an expectation of twenty enrolments, and to find two hundred pupils wishing to join. In any class it is vital that everyone should

(a) be able to see the teacher;
(b) have room to practise (about 40–50 square feet);
(c) have the teacher's personal attention for at least five minutes.

These three minimum requirements are quite outside the possibilities of the usual class, for practical reasons which will be dealt with later.

4. Many Yoga teachers have very small, excellently run private groups, or single pupils on an appointment basis. Here again, the idea is excellent, in fact to many it is the ideal: 'to every Yogi his own guru'. But a 'guru' with thirty private pupils each coming once a month will have no time to himself, for his own Yoga refreshment, let alone to enjoy life with his family and friends; and anyone having private pupils weekly can only afford to have three or four pupils.

5. There are other ways of learning: various combinations of methods 1 to 4, or occasionally residential or day courses, correspondence courses, and so on. But when all is said, the situation is still very serious. There is an acute shortage of experienced and well-qualified Yoga teachers: men and women who will come forward to meet what amounts to a need, a challenge, a problem and an opportunity. That is what this book is about. It is meant as an aid, an encouragement, a warning and a source of ideas to:

– those many people who are already teaching Yoga, without much experience, or any proper qualifications;
– qualified and experienced teachers who would like to evaluate their ideas and methods, and may find stimulation in these pages;
– those who are taking courses of training, either with Local

Education Authorities, or with the bodies in this country who offer training courses;

– teachers in schools: teachers of PE, drama, dance or RE who would like to extend their range of subjects;

– anyone connected with systems of therapy and relaxation, or any other subject which is related to Yoga;

– students in colleges and universities who would like to offer the subject as part of their teaching career;

– Local Education Authorities and other bodies who are running training courses, or intending to do so, and are needing a basic textbook.

It is necessary to say a few words about what the book does *not* presume to do: it is not the author's intention to provide another book about Yoga. This book is about how to *teach* Yoga, though clearly a great deal will have to be said about Yoga itself *en passant*.

It is not the author's intention to support any particular system of teaching Yoga. Various 'schools' exist, and the author would like to feel that his readers were led to think about or discuss with others the fact of the existence of 'schools' of Yoga teaching, and how far this should affect their own teaching.

How to use the book

Yoga itself naturally falls into eight parts, or 'limbs':

1. Control (*Yama* – the Sanskrit word used in the ancient classical texts of Yoga teaching). This comprises: non-violence, truthfulness, honesty, self-discipline, and generosity.
2. Attitudes (*Niyama*): a single-minded view of the world, contentment, self-discipline in dealing with others, self-knowledge, and an awareness of the deepest aspects of our lives as individuals and members of the created community.
3. Postures and movements (*Asanas*).
4. Breathing techniques (*Pranayama*).
5. Detachment of the mind from the senses (*Pratyahara*).
6. Concentration (*Dharana*).
7. Contemplation or meditation (*Dhyana*).
8. Union with the divine (*Samadhi*).

The teaching of Yoga, again, naturally falls into neat compartments:

1. The teacher himself:
   – his own Yoga expertise;
   – his knowledge of the subject: the eight 'limbs', the history of Yoga, and the philosophy on which it is based;
   – his knowledge of the working of the human mind and body;
   – the personal qualities he needs to commend his subject to his pupils;
   – his ability to demonstrate visually the things that are necessary in Yoga classes;
   – his ability to describe postures and movements, verbally;
   – his ability to lead his pupils in relaxation techniques and breathing sequences;
   – his ability to lead his class into a successful experience of concentration and contemplation;
   – his ability to project a 'warmth of character' to his class, so that the evening is a pleasant social occasion;
   – his knowledge of the extensive literature on the subject, which will enable him to advise about books and other aids.

2. The immense variety of needs which bring people to Yoga, and the maintaining of a proper balance between loyalty to the subject, and response to the pupils' needs.

3. Class management.

4. Certain optimum standards in teaching environment: space, time, temperature, furniture, equipment.

5. Safety rules in the room, in the class, and in the syllabus.

6. Teaching children and young people.

7. Teaching the sick, blind and deaf.

8. Private pupils.

Each of these topics needs as much space as the book will allow, together with illustrations where appropriate. And even then, we have only concerned ourselves with Hatha Yoga. There remain many other forms of Yoga, such as Raja

Yoga, Yjana Yoga, Karma Yoga, Bakhti Yoga, which are outside the scope of this book.

The advice of the author is that it may not be advisable to read the book through and lay it aside, but rather to have it to hand for ready reference. The chapters deal concisely with their topics.

There is also a list of suggestions for further reading at the end of the book: it is far too easy to spend money on attractive books which tend to present similar information in different words, and with different sets of illustrations. The photographic illustrations in this book are so arranged that they show how a teacher might present certain aspects of a few common postures. The book, to emphasise the point finally, is about *teaching method*. No one ought even to commence training for Yoga teaching without considerable experience of *doing* Yoga (or, ideally, *living* Yoga-style), so the readers of this book are assumed to have knowledge and experience. Those who have not are advised to turn straight to the suggestions for further reading!

2: The Teacher

The aim of this chapter is simple. It is to answer three questions:

1. What sort of people are Yoga teachers?
2. What sort of people *should* Yoga teachers be?
3. How can a Yoga teacher develop, to become something more akin to the ideal?

1. *What sort of people are Yoga teachers?*

The question may seem impertinent to the well-established teacher. But it is very relevant to the present situation, when many people are coming forward to meet the demand for more teachers. In any case, it is no bad thing for teachers to re-appraise themselves from time to time.

Recent experience of training newcomers to the profession suggests that it is best to resort to classification, though this has its pitfalls. So we will 'sort' the teachers into well-defined categories:

Background: Supposing that Yoga teaching is not their full-time occupation, what else do they do? The following is but a selection of backgrounds: school-teachers, secretaries, nurses, lecturers, housewives, retired people, students, therapists, workers in offices, and in industry. Many have other interests, and teach other subjects, apart from their full-time occupations: physical education, dance, drama, ballet, judo, karate, religious education. Many have interests which they share with others: transcendental meditation, hypnosis, modelling, fashion, slimming clubs, social work.

These people will have different views of the subject, and

we must take account of this in answering the third question, at the end of this chapter.

Sex: It cannot have escaped the notice of Yoga teachers and their pupils that, on average, ninety per cent of Yoga pupils are female, and about seventy per cent of Yoga teachers are female too. Here again, this is a mere observation, but it does have a bearing on the image of the subject and the way it might be taught. We shall also have to say something about the pros and cons of men teaching women, women teaching men and about mixed or single-sex classes.

Age: Age matters a good deal, regardless of other things. Youth has distinct advantages in some respects: many young teachers can 'command a following' by the sheer force of their personality, and their suppleness. But more mature teachers tend to find they can call upon the resources of their own experience of life to great effect, particularly in teaching relaxation, mental techniques, and the Yoga life-style.

Enthusiasm: Some will wonder whether this is ever in doubt. But where it is students are quick to notice 'lapses in concern'. It is surely agreed that it is not enough to do it 'just for the money'. Again, the enthusiasm may be there, but it may be unbalanced: keen about postures, unconcerned about meditation, for instance. So this must feature with the other considerations, in section 3 of the chapter.

Motives: Motives, for the purposes of this book, are those things that make a person decide to take up Yoga teaching, for example:

- response to a local call for more teachers;
- desire to share a personal enthusiasm;
- a wish to extend a career already based on teaching;
- a response by a relaxed and integrated person to the needs of a world in stress and confusion.

Aims: An aim is what stands at the far end of one's teaching of Yoga – an aim for oneself and an aim for the pupils: self-fulfilment; doing Yoga with others who are experienced, and helping them; the enjoyment of the stimulation of a session that goes well; the thrill of seeing many satisfied customers; making new friends; perfecting one's own Yoga; earning an honest penny to help support one's own reading, or the modest family budget.

Objectives: The establishment of accepted procedures with the class, of relaxation, breathing and posture techniques; the communication of Yoga attitudes; having at least a small number of pupils who have experienced something like an 'out-of-the-body-experience'. Other possible objectives will come to mind: helping a particular person who clearly has problems; getting to know the experienced Yogi in the back row, etc.

Physique and expertise: There are very great differences here, and these are reflected in the kind of Yoga that is taught. There is also the related question whether what is taught must be within the ability of the teacher, and an aspect of the subject in which he sincerely believes.

Clearly you do not have to be stunningly attractive or mightily fit to teach Yoga, nor do you need to have a repertoire of eighty-four postures before planning a year's work for beginners. But are there certain definitive guide-lines?

Mental capacity: An odd phrase perhaps, but it is difficult to describe very easily the varieties of mental calibre that teachers bring to their classes: the degree to which they are able to provide a challenge to the intellect of their pupils, or relate to those whose interest in the mental aspects of Yoga is minimal. Or again, it is important to ask whether it is essential to be intelligent, intellectual perhaps, in order to present the subject properly.

Knowledge of Yoga: Consider the areas of knowledge that could fairly be expected:

- human anatomy and physiology
- psychology
- postures, movements, breathing techniques

– the history and philosophy of Yoga
– the development of Yoga in this country
– methods of concentration, contemplation and meditation.

How far is standardisation necessary? Should you follow your own enthusiasm? Conform?

The ability to make personal relationships: Almost by definition, Yoga is a self-discipline, a private affair – essentially inward. How successful will a less experienced teacher be, especially one who has had no educational training, at communicating this intimate art to groups of the general public, probably averaging thirty per session at first, many of whom he will never get to know? Is there a need for an element of stagecraft, a sense of occasion?

Voice: The voice is part of the anatomy and is good, bad or indifferent. But teachers without experience, or without an honest class of confident, perhaps even outspoken pupils, may err in many directions: too slow, too fast, a bedside manner only heard by the front row, or a militant and strident sound unlikely to relax anyone. Is there any flexibility, any ebb and flow of voice power? Is the voice being used effectively, not only as an instrument of communication, as in direct instruction, but also as a substitute for the Inner Voice, as in relaxation and meditation?

Appearance, dress and manner: One of the things a Yoga teacher is there for is to be stared at! What do the class see? We can do a little, sometimes a great deal, to improve on nature! But sometimes woefully little is done to set an example of self-discipline. There is even, among some, a 'tradition of the unkempt' which is to be deplored. So much depends upon the class feeling that they can bear, not to say want, to watch their teacher standing, sitting, lying prone or supine, or performing postures, without averting their eyes from the dusty marks of last night's session at another centre, a split seam, uncared-for nails, and tired hair (not to mention evidence of strain in a face that is intended to induce stimulation to action and positive, pleasant rest!)

Life-style: The most impertinent pry of all! But to many class members, even beginners, 'learning Yoga' soon turns to 'living Yoga', and it is interesting to note how the teacher 'switches off' at the end of a class. Should the class see him (or her) reach for a cigarette before leaving the room? And there are other things that could be said, but are perhaps better left to the imagination!

2. *What sort of people should Yoga teachers be?*

What is offered here is merely a suggested 'table of things considered necessary'.

(a) Of course men and women, without distinction, can be excellent Yoga teachers. But in certain circumstances, one or the other might be preferred by the class. It may be that men are more likely to join a class if the teacher is a man, but this is not conclusively proven. The best kind of class is of mixed sexes and ages. But there are good reasons for having a 'ladies only' class, taken by a woman. There are very good reasons for having a men-only class taken by a man. The masculine elements in Yoga need to be stressed, perhaps more than they have been: the controls, uses of structured strength, and sustained balance; the special breathing techniques, and the many postures that are more congenial to men (and boys).

(b) Age is not a major point of contention, though experience most certainly is. Young Yoga teachers will endear themselves to their classes particularly if they are quick to draw on the greater experience of their pupils, especially in matters of Yoga life-style, or experience of contemplation, or breathing techniques.

(c) Generally speaking, background will influence the content of lessons, and the approach to the subject. Provided the teacher is aware of this, he (she) will make the right adjustment, and be ready to see other points of view. For instance, it may be that a physiotherapist finds Yoga very much akin to her work in hospital, but she must be prepared to present aspects of Yoga that are far removed from physiotherapy, without betraying any note of unfamiliarity or a hint that she finds them uncongenial.

gely because of the personal nature of the
ges of teachers due to sickness or other

s tried to draw the teacher's attention to
ths and weaknesses, and the opportunities
ait him; and to suggest that the long, cool
clear and practical ways of making the best

(d) Enthusiasm (motives, aims and objectives).

This is vital

The teacher's own personal enthusiasm will set the scene for the lesson, but must not dominate its content. His motive must be adaptable enough to be subservient to his aim. In other words, what moves him to take up Yoga teaching must merge, particularly during his time with the class, with his general aim – his purpose for the class. He may find it useful to pass on to the class his reasons for taking up teaching Yoga, but he should make it clear that these are secondary. His purpose, his aim for the class, will be:

– to give them a pleasant experience of relaxation;

– to provide them with opportunities to explore ways of making their bodies more supple, their minds more controlled;

– to present opportunities, which they may or may not wish to take up, of becoming familiar with the philosophy of Yoga, the claims that Yoga makes about the relationship of the mind, the body and the personality, and the deeper aspects of meditation;

– to introduce them to the Yoga way of life, without of course suggesting that it is obligatory to undertake it.

This is his long-term aim: his purpose, hopefully, for those who may take up the study of Yoga over many years.

His short-term objectives will depend very much upon himself, his class, and the conditions under which he and they are working together. Generally, it is best to provide a mixed menu of activities with the limited objective of allowing the pupils to taste and assess their liking for the subject in its various aspects. He should ask the class from time to time how they like their sessions, and invite them to make comments about their experience, to help him plan ahead. Groups differ quite startlingly in their approach: some will want relaxation and postures, other groups, usually small ones, will want and gain a great deal from concentration, meditation and discussion. So, to summarise this central theme:

– whatever a teacher's personal motive for taking up Yoga teaching, the needs of his class must take precedence;

– he will, must, have a long-term aim, which cannot be less than the presentation of the subject, in all its aspects;

– he will plan successive immediate objectives, basing them on the response of his class. In this, as in so much educational work, the 'customer' is more often right than we think!

(e) In order to cope successfully with everything from simple relaxation to sustained meditation, the teacher must have a certain minimum standard of basic health, suppleness, and intelligence. In view of the demands likely to be made upon him, it would clearly be to his advantage to have a degree of stamina, not only in order to survive a week's teaching which may involve three classes, perhaps fifty miles apart, but in order to respond positively to the emotional demands of the subject: the strain of imparting relaxation without becoming personally exhausted. He will gradually become familiar with the special language that has grown around the subject and with the ways of thinking, speaking and writing which characterise Yoga in the modern West. Certainly he cannot pretend to expertise if he is not well-read, either through laziness, lack of concentration, or the inability to absorb the meaning of what is written.

(f) It goes without saying that the teacher will know his subject, though what this entails is a matter deserving a chapter by itself. But it needs to be said that it is not sufficient to pass on to others only those aspects of Yoga that have provided the teacher with pleasure and benefit: he has a duty to the whole subject. He also has a duty to his pupils, and must know how they 'tick', physically, mentally and emotionally.

(g) He must be able to make a positive relationship with his class. In almost every case, they will be volunteers, paying for their classes, paying for his services, and if they find him unhelpful, ungenerous or unpleasant, they will withdraw themselves from the class, perhaps take their custom elsewhere, and certainly report and compare views about him, as a person, just as children do about their teachers in school. Voice and appearance are important, and are more susceptible to change and improvement than we think. It *is* possible to talk too much, or too little; to shout, or to whisper. One

infallibl
opinions
They
so do hav
are likely
derette or
life – practi
So to the

3. *How can a*
the ideal?

We are not di
ability to *teach.*

(a) Many readers
for the teaching
will be:
Lectures on the
Lectures on ana
Lectures on teac
Lectures and pra
management
Observation of goo
others
Teaching practice,
of the public.

(b) Teachers already in
not only because they pr
especially if they are resid
opportunities for the ex
especially if they are from

(c) Yoga teachers should f
can meet regularly for their

(d) Teachers will also wish t

(e) They will, finally, attend
practices, and observe the obv
being at their best every weel

suffer very badly, la
subject, from chan
reasons.

This chapter ha
himself: his streng
and pitfalls that a
look will result in
of his talents.

infallible solution to the voice problem is to ask for honest opinions from the class.

They will not be very willing to comment on appearance: so do have a full-length mirror handy, and remember that you are likely to meet your pupils in the supermarket, the launderette or the office. Don't let them catch you living a double life – practising the opposite of what you teach!

So to the inevitable final question:

3. *How can a Yoga teacher develop to become something akin to the ideal?*

We are not discussing Yoga expertise particularly, but the ability to *teach*.

(a) Many readers of this book will be attending training courses for the teaching of Yoga. Necessary elements in such courses will be:

Lectures on the whole nature of the subject
Lectures on anatomy, physiology and psychology
Lectures on teaching method, for each aspect
Lectures and practical work in lesson planning and class management
Observation of good (and moderate) teaching on the part of others
Teaching practice, with other students, and with members of the public.

(b) Teachers already in posts will benefit from short courses: not only because they provide time for reading and reflection, especially if they are residential, but also because they provide opportunities for the exchange of ideas and experiences, especially if they are from a variety of backgrounds.

(c) Yoga teachers should form local associations so that they can meet regularly for their mutual benefit.

(d) Teachers will also wish to keep themselves well read.

(e) They will, finally, attend constantly to their own Yoga practices, and observe the obvious rules that will ensure their being at their best every week in the Yoga session. Classes suffer very badly, largely because of the personal nature of the subject, from changes of teachers due to sickness or other reasons.

This chapter has tried to draw the teacher's attention to himself: his strengths and weaknesses, and the opportunities and pitfalls that await him; and to suggest that the long, cool look will result in clear and practical ways of making the best of his talents.

3: The Pupils

This chapter is about the many thousands of people who are enjoying Yoga, every day of the week, all over Britain. Who are they? Why do they come? What do they want? What do they expect?

We shall look at them under a number of headings:

1. Beginners: types, motives and aims.
2. Experienced and advanced groups.
3. Children and family groups.
4. Individuals of various sorts.

1. *Beginners*

At the beginning of the Evening Class session, usually in September, quite staggering numbers of people enrol for Yoga lessons. Often the numbers in classes increase further for two or three weeks. Then the numbers begin to subside, and by mid-October classes generally comprise those who have decided to 'make a go' of Yoga. It is as well perhaps that numbers do drop off, since fifteen is usually the best class size. Those who fall away would probably not benefit from continuing, though it will always be a concern to the teacher that the fall-off may be due to his reaction to the large numbers, or his manner in dealing with them. Perhaps large classes are their own undoing.

Be that as it may, who are the people who come to Yoga lessons? Can we see a pattern in their backgrounds? Are there 'Yoga' types? Experience shows that the following are among the reasons (motives) which bring pupils into Yoga classes:

To keep fit; to become more fit; to keep slim; to become more slim; to develop some aspect of their figure or physique; to increase their powers of concentration; to combat mental fatigue; to combat nervous tension; to ease emotional stress; to become more even-tempered; to become more self-confident; to combat shyness; to express themselves through bodily awareness; to learn ways of physical-aesthetic creativity; to give point and purpose to their lives; to learn how to spend leisure effectively; to learn new ways to express a longing for meaning in life; to enable themselves to express in Yoga a form of living; to lose themselves in the calmness and serenity of deep rest; to pass a pleasant evening; to satisfy curiosity; to ease a particular physical or mental condition; to give moral support to an enthusiastic but diffident friend; to seek a sublimation of sex; to enjoy themselves; to be absorbed in an activity which leaves no time or opportunity to think, let alone talk, about the routines of work and family life.

And so you face your first class, knowing that a fair selection of these motives are felt by those present. Which of these needs do you try to satisfy? Can you satisfy a fair number of them, perhaps even most of them, by providing a mixed menu of physical, mental and relaxation techniques? The position is not made easier by the fact that most of these people will probably not have thought very much about their motives anyway!

And what about necessary considerations like breathing difficulties, spine ailments, blood pressure, emotional instability, and many other things?

It would also be useful to know something about their background: what they do for a living; how old they are; have they had previous experience of Yoga? (It can be disconcerting to find, after several weeks, that you have in the class someone who has had many years' experience of visiting ashrams in India, and has kept quiet about it!)

We have not finished yet! In an LEA class, term often begins with the tiresome business of enrolments, and the collection of money: what do you do during this inevitable chaos?

Maybe the distribution of questionnaires is the answer. They can be filled in on the spot (remember to provide a possible fifty pencils!), and those who arrive late can return them the following week. Here is a suggested outline for a questionnaire:

Mr/Mrs/Miss
First name(s):
Surname:
Address:
Telephone number:
Year of birth:
Occupation:
Have you any previous experience of Yoga? How much?
What aspects of Yoga specially interest you? (Tick as many as you like):
- *Physical relaxation*
- *Breathing techniques*
- *Postures and movements*
- *Concentration and meditation*
- *Yoga philosophy*
- *Dieting*
- *The Yoga way of life*

Have you any special reason for coming to this Yoga class? Tick any of the following, or add your own reason underneath:
- *Physical fitness*
- *Improve figure*
- *Improve physique*
- *Nervous tension*
- *Emotional stress*
- *Interest in the whole subject*
- *Just relaxation*
- *Curiosity: I may not stay very long.*

Have you any of the following?
- *Tendency to breathlessness or asthma*
- *Spine ailments*
- *Blood pressure*
- *Anything else that might affect Yoga?*
- *Any further comments or questions.*

Note: This information is confidential to your Yoga teacher.

My suggestion is that you go through this list of questions with the class, allowing them to ask questions, or make comments. Let them use this experience to get used to you –

their teacher for the next twenty weeks or so, one hopes. Be informal, perhaps even hearty – the odd teasing remark: make them really at home – let them talk to each other. Set aside ten minutes at the end for the inevitable questions, enquiries: 'Do you think I should . . .?', 'Will there be any . . .?', 'I've never done . . .?', 'Can I bring a friend . . .?'

Before they disperse *make it quite clear* that the success of the *class*, quite apart from benefit to individuals, depends on certain simple rules:

1. Try to be punctual.
2. Keep the room warm: close doors and windows if you arrive early. Regulate heaters as appropriate for the weather and the time of year.
3. Yoga is in many ways very personal, private and intimate: respect other people's privacy, respect their choice of activity, don't disturb the class during silence.

For the best results, each pupil should:

(a) Wear loose clothing: ladies should wear leotards, or jumpers and shorts, but bring warm, extra garments, especially for relaxation. Men should wear shirts and shorts, again with extra garments for relaxation.

(b) Very few centres will have the luxury of fitted carpets, or mats provided. So bring a mat. (A blanket or a towel is really not enough, either in size or thickness.) Some mats for Yoga are available commercially, but less expensive floor covering can often be obtained in adequately sized offcuts.

(c) Try not to have a large meal less than two hours before the session. Coffee or tea afterwards, especially if the centre has a snack-bar, can be very pleasant indeed – and an added social occasion.

In the second week, report on the questionnaires (in general terms, of course) and promise to provide for their expressed needs as far as possible. Suggest perhaps that absolute beginners may like to sit at the back, and gain from the experience of watching the others. Try to establish a tradition whereby the business of changing, before and afterwards, is part of the session: a time for changing moods as well as clothes, for greeting friends and establishing the best social atmosphere.

What do you do if there are 100 in the class? You can reckon on a twenty-five per cent loss over the first four weeks, so the best way out would be to split the class: ask some to come, say at 7 pm, and the others at 8.30. It will make a three-hour session for the teacher, with groups of thirty-five or so for many weeks. If this is too many, then there may be another room, and another teacher handy, but usually, at the moment, this is like asking for the moon!

Don't forget to *try* to do some actual Yoga, even on that first hectic evening, even if it's only some simple standing movements, breathing routines, and a little relaxation.

2. *Experienced and advanced groups*

Towards the end of the session, the class begins to present a new problem. If you have been successful, there will be many who will want to continue for another year, and yet you know already that there will be a considerable number coming fresh to the subject when the new session begins. What should you do? There are several alternatives:

(a) Keep the experienced people together, and start a new class for absolute beginners.

(b) Let beginners join the existing class or classes, and learn from the rest as well as from yourself.

(c) Estimate your own talents, and if you think it advisable (and if it is possible) bring in a second teacher, either for the experienced group, or the absolute beginners.

But what does 'experience' mean? What is an 'experienced' pupil? He could be any of the following:

(a) Someone who is supple and strong, who has mastered every posture and technique in your first twenty-week course, and wants to break new ground next year.

(b) Someone who has made some headway with a fair number of postures, but is a little bored, and wants something different now.

(c) Someone who has made considerable progress with postures, has become interested in meditation, and wants to begin all over again, and 'do everything properly' next year. No new material – just doing last year's work with greater concentration, greater benefit, and more lasting pleasure. And there are other kinds too.

There is a lot to be said for letting a class continue on the same evening – staying together as a cohesive group, especially if group meditation has been a feature of later sessions. A few newcomers will probably enjoy joining a group which is already a friendly, sociable one.

But if there is a group of, say, a dozen, who really want to forge ahead, they should be given the chance to do so. Twelve can often meet in ideal surroundings – a small draught-free room tucked away from noise and disturbance. If this group comprises persons of maturity and responsibility, they might well be left now and then to devise their own programme of activities, with one of their number acting not as a leader so much as a liaison between them and the teacher. If so, they should meet when the teacher is available for queries and 'guest appearances'.

3. *Children, and family groups*

Working with young children will have a chapter to itself in due course. Teenage children, coming with their parents, or parents accompanying teenagers, present no great problem, in fact it is much to be encouraged, for it shows a kind of family cohesion which we rarely see these days, and the session will provide conversation for them at home, between lessons.

Children under ten need rather different treatment, even if their parents attend with them. They must be prepared to spend their time co-operating in a programme designed for children, as opposed to 'family Yoga'. That is not to say that parents are not welcome: on the contrary, there is something quite delightful about a mother and her two or three children – among them perhaps a toddler of only three or four – enjoying an hour's Yoga and then going home and trying it all over again – perhaps even getting father, and granny to join in!

4. *Individuals of various sorts*

These 'special cases' often provide the greatest problems, and sometimes the greatest satisfaction. They must not be allowed to distract your attention from the great majority, who come along each week, enjoy their Yoga session, and go home again, without perhaps even having a thought that they could or should 'have a word with' the teacher!

We will introduce a few 'special cases', in person: by giving them a question to ask, or a request to make, or a comment or criticism, and then we will provide a short, positive answer.

1. 'I know I have missed eight weeks, but I have only just moved into the area, and my neighbour told me I could come.'
Answer: 'It's a pleasure to have you in the class. Would you like to sit with your friend, at the back, then you can watch the others and no one will see you. You'll soon pick up the idea. Ask for a questionnaire before you go, and see the registrar about your fee and enrolment.'

2. 'I'm sorry: we're moving next week to Scotland.'
Answer: 'Have you enjoyed yourself? We shall miss you. Can I put you in touch with a group in Scotland? Leave me your new address and I'll send you the name of your nearest teacher. Come and see us again if you are passing through.'

3. 'Can I bring a friend?'
Answer: 'Yes, of course: there seem to be some odd spaces here and there. Introduce him/her to me when we meet next week.'

4. 'Do you have a waiting list, or can I just join now?'
Answer: 'We don't have 'waiting lists': we try to fit everybody in: so I should fill a space over there while you can!'
(People on waiting lists usually go to something else, so there's little point in keeping newcomers out on their account.)

5. 'I'd like to join, but tell me, are there any men in the class?'
Answer: 'I expect there will be about one man to every ten women. You are very welcome to join: why don't you give it a week's trial?'
(Difficult to know why they ask this question, unless it's a man, and it's obvious he doesn't want to be the only one!)

6. 'These postures just aren't for me: I'm too bottom-heavy. I think I'd better stop.'
Answer: 'You're doing very well – there are lots of things to

choose from: just do the things you like. You don't have to join in everything. Yoga isn't like any other class: you just do what you like.'

7. 'I just want to meditate: do I have to do postures?'
Answer : 'You may be lucky, but most people find that relaxation and meditation come easier after about thirty or forty minutes of physical work, and breathing exercises. If you can't stand postures, just sit in the corner: but I think you may find it interesting to meditate *in* postures: use the postures themselves for meditation.'

8. 'I'm not really interested in this philosophy and meditation you tell us about every week.'
Answer : 'Well, I'm always careful to say that not everybody agrees with it. I suggest that you use the time for quiet relaxation, and join in again for the final posture session. I teach the whole subject – not only because these classes are advertised as Yoga classes, but also because I'm interested in the whole subject too.'

9. 'What about diet?'
Answer : 'I shall be talking about diet and other things like that after the first four or five weeks. Meanwhile, I suggest that you try eating a little less, and a lot less on Yoga nights!'

10. 'I have been on sedatives: should I give them up?'
Answer : 'You must ask for your doctor's advice. But I hope that you will find that Yoga may help you to do without drugs.'

11. 'Why are there so few men?'
Answer : 'I think there are two main reasons: (i) Women got there first and men are afraid to enter what has become very much a feminine empire; (ii) Many men are too impatient for Yoga: they'd rather kick, throw or strike a ball. They're more interested in active, often violent, sports. But there's a great deal in Yoga that demands masculine strength and control. In time, the balance will gradually even out, I'm sure.'

12. 'Do you take private classes? Would you accept me as a private pupil?'
Answer : 'Why do you want special tuition? Don't you feel

that the class is helping you? I don't usually have private pupils, and you must realise that I would have to charge you the same fee, at least, that I get from class teaching. I would be willing to take you on for a trial period. Telephone me to make an appointment, we will discuss a programme of Yoga for you, and if it helps you, you can make another appointment about a month later.'

13. 'I've just spent ten years in India: this is not the Yoga I learned there.'
Answer: 'Yoga is rather different in the West. I hope you will find it pleasant and helpful. If not, you should try to visit an oriental teacher: there are some, especially in London.'

14. 'Will Yoga help me to extend my powers of control over objects, and over other people?'
Answer: 'I'm not sure whether you have this power. Yoga is not intended to be used in this way. What Yoga *will* do, if you let it, is to make you a balanced, integrated person. That may increase the powers you say you have. Let me know.'

There are lots of other questions that could be asked, and often are. This is only a selection of the most common ones. Others will be dealt with during the course of the remaining chapters.

Certainly it is vital to get to know the pupils well: get round to using surnames as soon as possible, and later on, to first names. Discussion every so often will become routine, and they will come prepared to talk.

As in all teaching, you are wasting your time if you are not connecting with your class.

4: Somewhere to Teach

A tour of Yoga classes in any part of Britain reveals quite staggering extremes in what educationalists call the 'teaching environment'. We will imagine several such cases, which will probably be in keeping with the experience of many students and their teachers. I hasten to point out that no unkindness is intended here, only the wish to be realistic. We can do a great deal to improve on existing working conditions, but we first have to be aware of their faults.

1. A class of twenty beginners in an infant school hall, on the ground floor. Probably the main corridor opening into, and out of it. High ceiling. Radiators, parquet floor. Tall windows. Faults: changing facilities and furniture too small. Comings and goings of other classes. Severe through-draughts. Minimum temperature at floor level. Convection currents near radiators. Fixed lighting. Over-resonant room. Floor surface difficult to prepare between the end of school and the arrival of the class. Windows liable to faults in their mechanism: difficult to close a faulty window without assistance. Unwanted and unwelcome faces and voices at the windows. Noise of other classes. Teacher must choose to use high stage, or no raised platform at all.

2. Thirty experienced students in a modern gymnasium. School proud of its gym, and class initially pleased to have the use of it, and the tumbling mats as well. But there are agreed limits to gymnasium heating: agreed *minimum* temperatures. Yoga is thought to be an active pastime, and in consequence the room is at the wrong temperature for relaxation and meditation. High ceiling doesn't help. But the changing facilities are excellent.

3. A dozen students and their teacher meet in a village community centre. The floor has a fitted carpet, the room is warm, just large enough, and has a low ceiling, with easily controlled lights. The teacher doesn't need a platform. The only sounds are from the adjacent kitchen, where snacks and coffee are served to other users of the centre.

4. Forty-five beginners crowd into a largish room in a technical college. Quiet and warm, a platform for the teacher, and some mats provided. But at 8 pm ordered chaos takes over, for coffee is served from 8 till 8.30, and classes take a break. The Yoga class must decide whether to conform, or soldier on. Certainly no relaxation or meditation can take place whilst well-intentioned students of car maintenance or flower arrangement, or thirsty badminton players, flock past outside the door. Then at 9 pm a bell rings around the building, summoning night shift cleaners to begin sweeping up, and the class must dismiss without ceremony in the face of incoming brooms, or mechanical polishers.

So to the task of laying down some optimum requirements by way of teaching environment, equipment and materials.

First, the pupil himself (see Diagram 1). If he is about 5 ft. 8 ins. tall, then he is likely to need about fifty square feet of space in order to perform adequately without colliding with his neighbour. Such an occurence might cause offence (or perhaps a budding friendship, but that is irrelevant to our purpose here!). This also means that if he is to have some comfort throughout the session, he should ideally have a mat 7 ft. 6 ins. × 7 ft. 6 ins. It would be quite out of the question for a centre to provide these, but pupils could bring their own, and have them stored on the premises.

Then: how to group the class (see Diagram 2). First there is the 'serried ranks' version (A): about the only possible one with very large numbers, but unless the teacher has a platform he will not be seen beyond the second or third row.

Secondly there is the 'radiating rows' arrangement (B). This is much the best with the moderately sized class. All eyes can be on the teacher and he can do so much more than merely demonstrate and hope for the best. He can visually

Diagram 1 The space required for one Yoga pupil is 50 square feet at least

A.

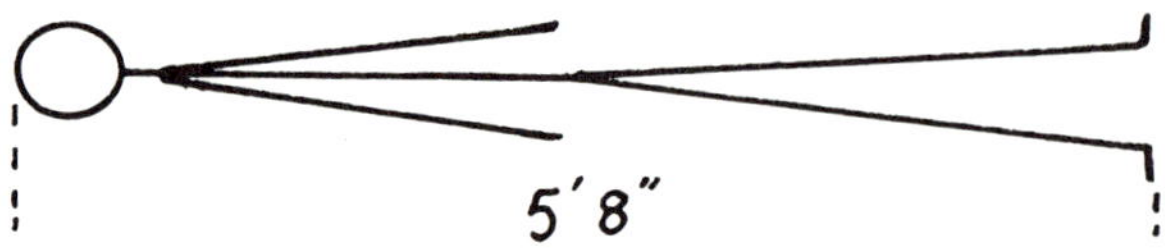

B.

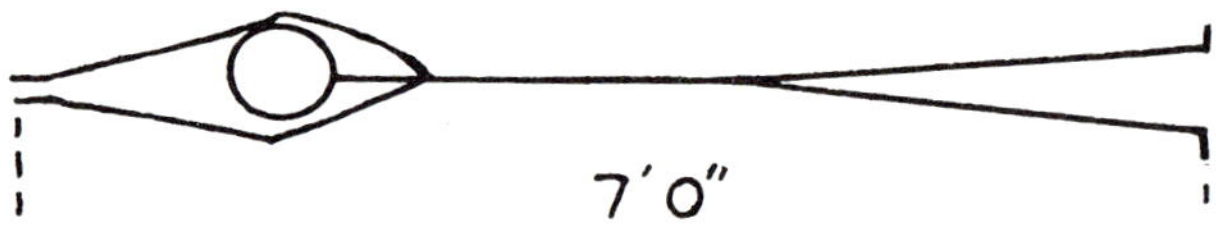

C.

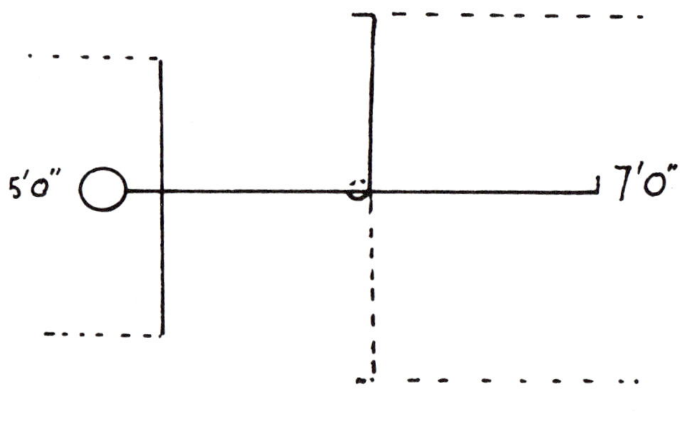

D.

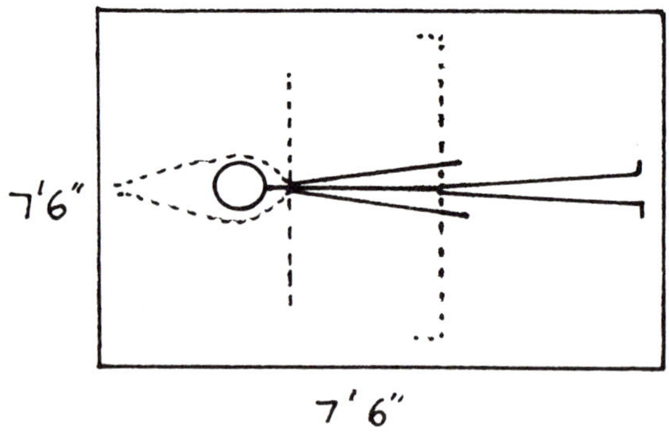

Diagram 2 How to arrange a class

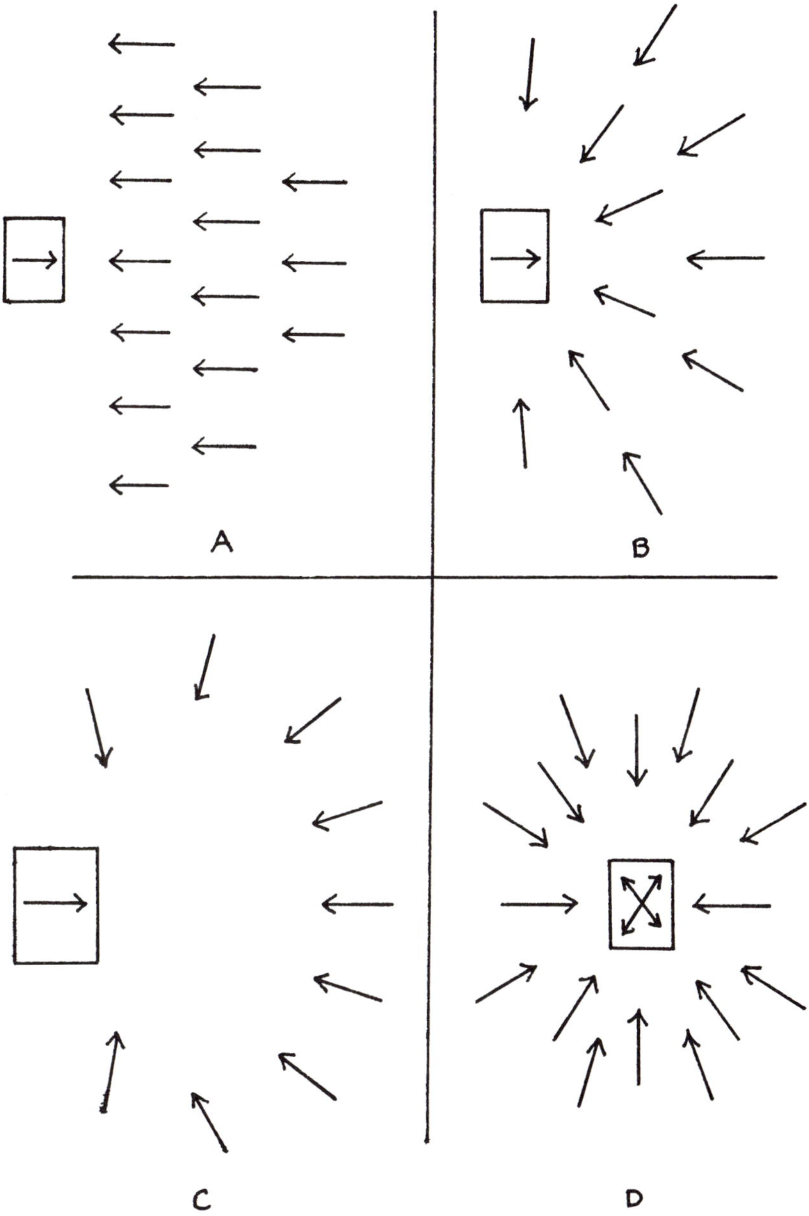

'link' with each pupil, and even convey visual messages which don't disturb the others, but make everyone feel 'noticed'.

Thirdly, the teacher may sit in a circle with his pupils, and will probably not need a platform (C). This is ideal for the small, informal group, and much the best for meditation, especially candle meditation and similar exercises.

Lastly, he may sit in the centre of the room, with his pupils all around him (D). This poses problems: he will never be seen or heard well by more than half the class, but it has the advantage, especially where demonstration is the order of the day, that the postures (which, like sculpture, need to be seen from every angle) can be shown to the best effect. Perhaps it is not irreverent to suggest a revolving platform, especially for the full Spine Twist!!

Heat, light and sound

Limbering movements, structured routines, the Salute to the Sun, held postures, slow controlled breathing, recollected relaxation and a self-forgetful meditation: all these can, perhaps *should*, happen in any one Yoga session. Each one needs a different quality of heat, light and sound.

Heat: It *must* be warm. It must *not* be stuffy. There *must* be good ventilation. But, please, *no* draughts.

So we might suggest the following. The Yoga room, from the point of view of the best kind of heating,

- should be upstairs;
- should be at least two doors removed from outside access;
- should have a wooden floor;
- should be big enough for forty persons at 50 square feet each, i.e. thirty persons plus space for the teacher, and perhaps a demonstrator. This works out at a staggering 2250 square feet, approximately. Clearly, it could be done in a smaller space, but we are dealing here with definitive standards;
- should have a low ceiling, and standard sized, but normal height windows: i.e. the sills at 3 ft. above the floor;
- should have silent, non-convective heating: preferably the

rather old-fashioned radiators, with manually operated controls on each unit;
– should face south or west, to ensure the best benefits from afternoon and evening sunshine. (If you teach in a building that has convecting heating and individually fused units, carry a pack of 13 amp fuses. It has been known for teachers to go round replacing fuses that have disappeared into teenagers' pockets during day school hours!)

Light: The class must be able to see the teacher, and the demonstrator, and the teacher must have a clear view of them, not only when he is teaching from the dais, but when he is moving about coaching and answering questions. On the other hand, in the Corpse Posture it is unpleasant to stare up into bright lights. Curtains at the windows in winter will effectively kill natural convection draughts, but will shut out natural light. All that is needed is separate controls for each light, or pair of lights. An added sophistication would be a fading device, which could be fitted to a standard lamp, and the lamp could then be used in many ways, in teaching and enjoying the uses of light in mind Yoga. This would be especially effective if the curtains provided complete blackout.

One small point, for note by the teacher. If you *have* to read your meditation notes, or you want to read from the Gita, or from Patanjali, for instance, bring a small battery-lamp, rather than using room lights. I say *lamp* because I mean a free-standing light rather than a torch, which you have to wave about, or even hold between your teeth whilst turning a page, which makes evenness of speech a little difficult!

What about wall-lights in our purpose-built centre . . .?

Sound: I am not concerned here about the teacher's own voice. I am concerned about the acoustics of the room, and other sounds, conducive to relaxation or positively distracting. Sound, like light, can be incorporated into Yoga: there is a great deal of real pleasure to be gained from listening to sounds objectively, and not as distractions: peoples' distant voices, traffic, receding footsteps, the ebb and flow of strong breezes, and the sounds of nature. But not ribald remarks from the street below, the strivings of a teacher who is not doing very well in the room next door, rattling tea-cups and the not uncommon, if clearly necessary, flushing of cisterns! Not to mention the clanging of alarm bells for various purposes not connected with the class, and the occasional disco – and what about squeaky doors? Every Yoga teacher should carry a small can of oil: just a few drops make all the difference.

A room such as we are beginning to have in mind will probably have few problems where noise is concerned, and in any case, a class will usually become accustomed to noise very quickly. But certain sounds are both distracting and unnecessary and a word with the appropriate person, with every diplomatic charm in the book, will often solve a problem that was not even known: 'Good heavens: why didn't you tell me . . .!'

Furniture and equipment

In most cases, if not all cases (where LEA classes are concerned at least) the room will be used for other purposes. So we have furniture in the room to dispose of before the class can start: either desks, tables, chairs, a grand piano (or an upright) – or we may be in a gymnasium and have to step warily, without shoes, taking care to leave existing equipment alone: ropes, bars, beams and perhaps a trampoline, or netball equipment.

Ideally, we need only the following (supposing there are good changing facilities):

1. A platform for the teacher and/or demonstrator. Clearly this will have to be at least 7 feet square, for the best effect, with a mat or carpet to match; high enough for all to see, but not so high that details, for instance of foot or knee positions at floor level, cannot be seen. This raises a point which we shall have to return to in the chapter on method: that there are many good reasons for gathering the class closely around the platform during demonstration – so many postures need to be viewed from above as well as from the side, if not more so. I would never encourage a teacher to use the stage in an assembly hall – it is too high and too remote.

2. Mats for everyone. If they bring their own then do encourage really sensible and useful mats: thick enough for

comfort, thin enough for firm stability, specially in balancing postures: smooth upper surface to allow movement, floor-hugging under-surface to prevent crinkling. And, if possible, full-size. If we have to compromise on size, then length is more important than width. The teacher should be able to keep a full-sized (6 ft. × 6 ft. at least) mat, for himself, on the premises. Any mats that are kept on the premises should be stacked flat if possible, pile to pile, to prevent their getting dirty.

3. A few chairs, or shelves, or cupboard tops, for additional clothing as and when needed, i.e. for jumpers, to put on for relaxation, and for shoes, spectacles, watches, etc.

4. A place, at a convenient height, for registers, a display of books perhaps, or other literature.

5. The teacher should have his own changing facilities. This is not to be in any sense discriminating, but the class would expect it and the teacher deserves it.

A purpose-built Yoga centre (see Diagram 3)

This idea may seem unrealistic, but such a centre might be incorporated into a sports complex, or Health Centre. In any case, there is no harm in indulging in a little fancy as to what one could do with unlimited funds.

Diagram 3 needs virtually no further explanation. Perhaps it is sufficient to point out some of the features:

1. The working and the open aspects of the building face south.
2. The entrance steps suggest that the whole building (which is all on one level) should be several feet above ground level.
3. A double entrance hall means that the circulating area will be cosy: suitable as a reading, chatting and meeting room.
4. Proper changing, shower and powder-room facilities will encourage pupils to come in ordinary clothes, and change completely on arrival. So often it is necessary for a compromise which is 'un-Yoga', often unhealthy, and sometimes uncomfortable.

Diagram 3 A purpose-built Yoga centre

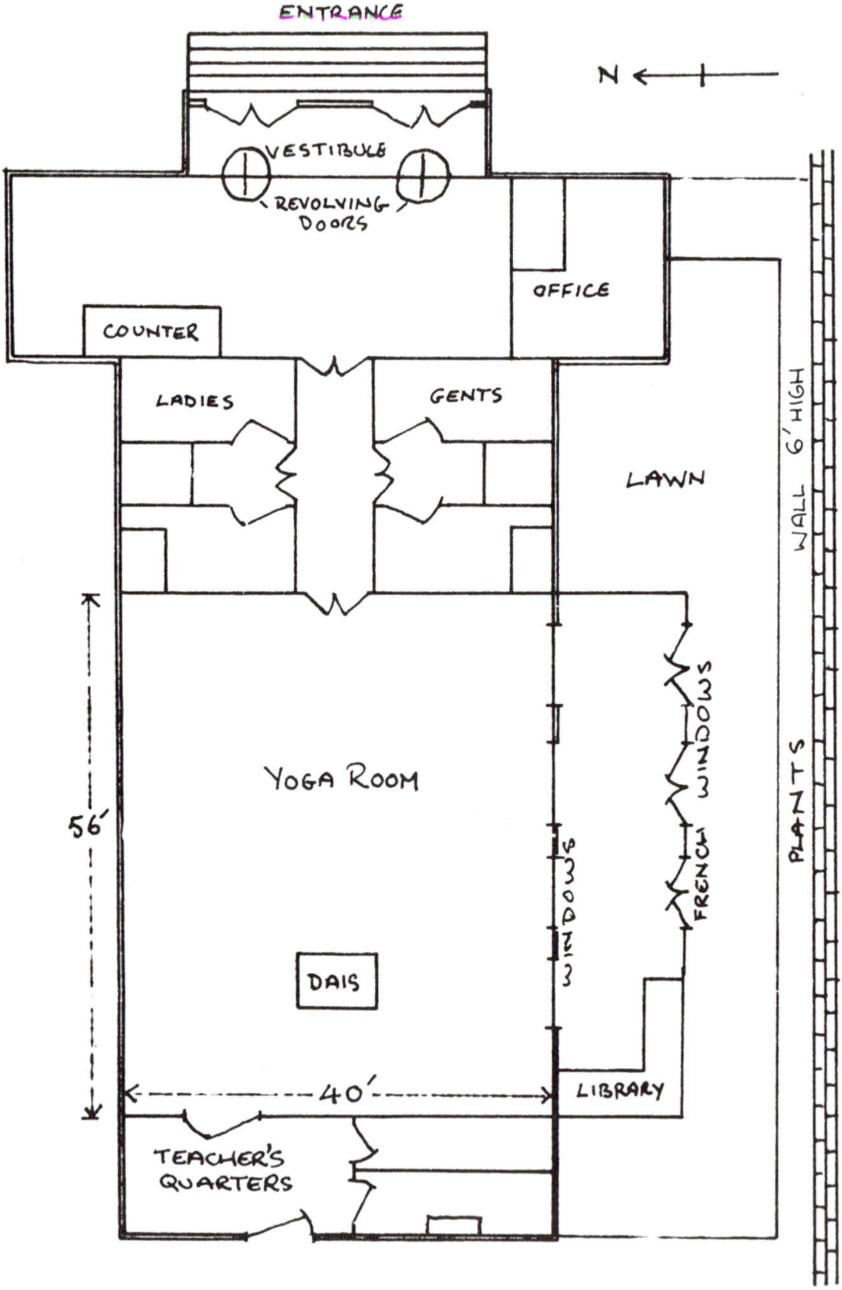

5. The tutor has his own facilities, and can retire, reappear etc. from his end of the group room.
6. A sort of conservatory, with French windows, leading to grounds outside makes open-air Yoga possible, given the right weather. The brick wall, at 6 feet, would be expensive, but would give privacy, and a good background for plants.

5: Planning a Course

Is this necessary, or advisable? Some teachers are convinced that you must take your cue from the class, basing next week's material on their response this week. Others are concerned to present Yoga in all its aspects. We are faced with three ways ahead:

Do we give the class what they most enjoy?

Do we give the class what they most need?

Do we give them Yoga, entire, regardless of their needs or enjoyment?

We are back to square one: aims, objectives and strategy. Our aim, unless curbed by official politics beyond our control, or by the expressed title of the course, is to present the whole of Yoga, over a period of time.

So planning is vital. Planning is not riding roughshod over class reactions; it is learning from experience how to prepare, in outline, at least a year in advance, the kind of ground that is to be covered.

We shall begin modestly, with ideas for an eight-week course, and then consider plans for a year, and for three years. We ought to say something, too, about day-seminars and residential weekends.

An eight-week course

Eight weeks? What can you do in eight weeks? It's not at all uncommon for a centre, especially an LEA centre, to hold a summer eight-week course. Many centres who cannot get teachers in September find that certain teachers are available in May and June because some of their own classes have ceased or have been combined with others.

To meet a group of beginners for the first time, in May, and give them an eight-week 'sampler', which often leads to a permanent class beginning in the following September, is a very pleasant way of spending the warm spring and summer evenings. But it does provide, on a very small scale, an exercise in planning. It can only be a 'sampler' but it must be done properly.

It is best to write down two lists of headings, and keep them handy each week, as a guide. We all know them, but I offer no apologies for repeating them.

(a) The eight limbs:

1. *Yama:* getting on with other people.
2. *Niyama:* coming to terms with yourself.
3. *Asana:* postures and movements.
4. *Pranayama:* breathing techniques.
5. *Pratyahara:* detachment from the world.
6. *Dharana:* concentration – steadying the mind.
7. *Dhyana:* contemplation – mindless attention.
8. *Samadhi:* bliss, which defies description.

The eight-week plan *must* relate in some way to these eight limbs, and even then it is only one branch of Yoga.

(b) The proper ingredients of Yoga lessons:

1. Limbering up: getting physically, mentally and emotionally into the mood of the evening.
2. Relaxation: deliberately dismissing control, step by step, of body, mind, emotions.
3. Breathing techniques.
4. Movements and postures.
5. Mental Yoga: use of light and sound; concentration; contemplation; silent meditation.
6. Yoga philosophy, history, ethics and life-style.
7. Discussion.
8. Free time: for individual Yoga, for coaching, for getting to know the class, and for being available for questions and discussion with individual class members.
9. Registration, money matters, literature, Yoga world news.
10. The unforeseen emergency or opportunity.

For eight weeks we must insist on two hours, say 7 pm –

9 pm. Encourage prompt arrival, and keep them at it until 8.55 pm! No break, apart from five minutes in the middle, for all administrative matters and notices.

Diagram 4 shows a suggested layout. Each week's work is set out under precisely defined headings, and a number of minutes is allocated to each. The headings ensure the proper spread of activities, and the minute allocation (total 120 minutes) gives a timed programme for each evening.

Here are some notes, and general thoughts about the scheme.

(a) *Week 1*. No time wasted on introductions: get them into Yoga before they have time to be self-conscious, or put up emotional barriers. Remember: many have come out of curiosity, and preliminary remarks may have an adverse effect, however well chosen!

Postures and movements: there are too many here to do properly, but make it clear that this is only a potted introduction, and they would do well to come to another class in the autumn to have the chance to begin again, without perhaps the handicap of mistaken preconceptions. Introduce meditation without any fuss, no suggestion that this is special in any way.

During discussion just ask for yes/no answers about what they liked most, and whether they think they'll find time to do some practice.

Try to have some hand-outs for them:

- perhaps a copy of the eight-week scheme;
- certainly a résumé of Week 1, with pin-men, and simple advice;
- questionnaires (see Chapter 3) to fill in at home, and return next week.

They may not want free time the first week, but they will appreciate revision of the postures.

Finally: praise for everyone, whatever their age. Don't give undue attention to individuals, but do expect the following week's turn-up to be different: of the thirty in the first week, about five will drop out, and if you have been a good teacher (whatever that means!), there will be five new ones, who missed Week 1.

Week	*Limbering work 5 mins*	*Relaxation 10 mins*	*Breathing 10 mins*	*Yoga movements and postures 45 mins*	*Light and sound 5 mins*	*Mental Yoga : concentration, contemplation, meditation 20 mins*	*Discussion 10 mins*	*Free 20 mins*
1	Standing, breathing	Using Corpse posture (i)	Abdominal	*Seated postures :* Cross-legged (Lotus); Twist; Shoulder stretch (Fish); Head to knee	Steady eye focus	Self-observation (1) Breathing sensations		Free for personal practice
2	Work with arms	Using Corpse posture (ii)	Diaphragm	*Supine postures :* Plough; Shoulder stand; Hip Twist; Ejector	Candle gazing	Self observation (2) Limb-consciousness		Free for personal practice
3	Work with legs	Using Prone position	Full Yoga Breath (i)	*Prone Postures :* Cobra; Bow; Locust; Cobra twist	Eye exer-cises	Candle gazing and retained images		Free for personal practice
4	Balancing	Seated	Full Yoga Breath (ii)	*Kneeling postures :* Child; Camel; Fencer; Swan; Head of Cow; Supine pelvic	Pos-tures with eyes closed	Self-observation 'mindfulness'		Free for personal practice
5	Head movements	Seated (on chairs)	Bellows etc.	*Standing postures :* Dancer; Tree; Standing twist; Tree; Backward arch; Chest stretch	Steady listen-ing	'Retreat from surround-ings'		Free for personal practice
6	Other methods (experi-ment)	Other methods (experi-ment)	Breathing in postures	'*All-fours' postures :* Cat; stomach lift; modified head stand	Direct-ed listen-ing	Other methods: experiment		Free for personal practice
7	Other methods (experi-ment)	Other methods (experi-ment)	Revision: Yoga breathing	*Revision :* Postures with breathing	Use of incense	Other methods: experiment		Free for personal practice
8	Other methods (experi-ment)	Other methods (experi-ment)	Revision: Breathing in postures	*Revision :* Grouping postures in sequences	Revi-sion	Other methods: experiment		Free for personal practice

(b) *Week 2*. Some references back to Week 1 are essential, and we haven't made any allowance for it in the plan. It could come in free time, or some of the new postures may have to be jettisoned.

There is a considerable body of opinion in support of a very limited range of activities, on the grounds that whatever is worth doing is worth doing slowly, seven times! Certainly, according to the apparent interests of the class, it is better, in Week 2, to do the Plough and Hip Twist well, with revision of the Spine Twist and Shoulder Stretch. This means that you will have to jettison the Shoulder Stand and the Ejector. There is no harm in this. The selection is there to aid the teacher's choice. The important thing is to keep to the general theme, whilst 'thinning out' the content a little. And this will apply throughout the course. Once again, don't forget the hand-outs. One of the real difficulties for beginners is remembering how to do postures and breathing techniques. It is not until a posture becomes almost second nature that the pupil can allow it to be a means to Yoga-ends. Whilst he is still striving to remember what to do next he will not find any noticeable benefit. Warn the class of this, lest you lose some who were hoping for immediate miracles.

Candle gazing: at first the group should be invited (not obliged) to group in a circle round a tall, safe, candle, brought by the teacher. Later, those who wish can bring their own to use in free time, *at their own risk*.

(c) *Weeks 3 – 6*. As the weeks proceed, many will feel, and the more confident will say, that they are not making 'progress' (they aren't likely to know how to recognise progress, because they won't know what to expect.) Make the point that in two months you can only *introduce* them to what the subject offers, and encourage them to devote three terms to following up this preliminary course during the ensuing season. This will apply, or should do, to all the aspects of the subject. As the final week approaches, devote some time to revision: many of them need to be reminded of movements and techniques. If you didn't give out copies of the scheme at the beginning (or even if you did), give out copies of a summary of the ground you have covered.

(d) During the last two weeks stress, gently but firmly, the importance of the first two 'limbs' which are taken to be prerequisites for any class. They *should* be more even-tempered with each other, more patient with themselves.

A Year's Work in Yoga

Make no mistake: a year (34 weeks for some Local Education Authorities, 24 for others; 40 weeks or more in private classes) will not do so very much more than eight weeks. But there certainly will be differences:

1. After the first month, the group will settle for about 20 weeks, and this is when most of the work will be done. The last ten weeks will see a falling-off, and a chance to do some small-group work with the remainder.

2. You will get to know the class well, unless there are forty in it, in which case you will get to know about half of them well!

3. They will see progress and benefits beginning to appear and will want to advise you with regard to adjusting the content of the sessions, to suit their particular needs. Unfortunately these 'needs' are not universal, sometimes not even those of the majority!

I would strongly advise against covering very much more ground than I have set out in the 8-week scheme. The 34-week scheme will show how I suggest the material might be divided up (Diagrams 5–7). It is based on the normal three-term arrangement adopted by most Local Education Authorities, except that by no means all Authorities have a summer session. Usually there are about twelve weeks before Christmas, twelve between Christmas and Easter, and ten in May, June and July. The scheme is suitable for ninety-minute sessions or for two-hour sessions, with only slight adjustments.

I do not propose that we take these schemes in detail, but merely offer a few notes by way of explanation.

(i) The order of postures and techniques is intended to follow a natural development of suppleness, and of growing acquaintance with the subject.

(ii) The postures and techniques are all within the scope of a beginners' group. I do not mean by this that they should all be perfected, but that most members of the class will be able to make a good beginning.

Diagram 5 A year's work in Yoga: (a) Autumn

Weeks	*Limbering exercises*	*Routines (see text)*	*Relaxation*	*Breathing*	*Posture revision*	*Mental work and meditation*	BREAK	*'Quickies' (see text)*	*New posture*	*Free time, discussion*
1	Standing Breath	1	Corpse	Abdomen	(Cobra)	Corpse: Thinking about breathing		Work with eyes	Child	
2	Standing Breath	1	Corpse	Abdomen	Cobra; Child	Corpse: Limb consciousness		Simple balance	Bow	
3	Standing Breath	1	Corpse	Diaphragm	Bow	Corpse: Mind consciousness		Squat and Kneel	Head to Knee	
4	Forward Droop	1	Corpse	Diaphragm	Head to Knee	Corpse: Emotion consciousness		Cobra Twist	Plough Lifts	
5	Backward Arch	2	Seated	Shoulders	Plough Lifts	Seated: Candle Gazing		Cat	Plough	
6	Droop and Arch	2	Seated	Shoulders	Plough	Seated: Candle Gazing		Modified Head stand	Plough Balance	Discussion of progress
7	Leg side Raise	2	Prone	Yoga Breath	Plough Balance	Prone: evocation of objects		Modified Head stand	Backstretches (1)	
8	Leg side Raise	2	Prone	Yoga Breath	Backstretches 1	Prone: evocation of objects		Half Crab	Backstretches (2)	
9	Standing Breath	3 (Mudras)	Own Choice	Yoga Breath	Backstretches 2	Own Choice: The Yoga Way of Life (1)		Crab	Backstretches (3) (Supine Pelvic)	
10	Droop and Arch	3 (Mudras)	Own Choice	Bellows	Backstretches 3 (Supine Pelvic)	Own Choice: The Yoga Way of Life (2)		Alternate arm and leg stretch	Dancer	
11	Leg side raise	1	Own Choice	Abdomen; Diaphragm; Shoulders	Dancer	Own Choice: The Yoga Way of Life (3)		Alternate arm and leg stretch	Dancer King	
12	Standing Breath	2	Revision	Yoga Breath	Revision	Own Choice: The Yoga Way of Life (4)		Revision	Revision	Suggestions: next term?

Diagram 6 A year's work in Yoga: (b) Winter – Spring

Weeks	*Limbering exercises*	*Routine (see text)*	*Relaxation*	*Breathing*	*Posture Revision*	*Mental work and relaxation*	BREAK	*'Quickies' (see text)*	*New posture*	*Free time, discussion*
1	Arm swings	1	Slow arm movements	Normal but timed	Dancer King	Own Choice: a Journey		Held Flop	Shoulder Stand (1)	
2	Arm swings	1	Slow arm movements	1.4.2	Shoulder Stand (1)	Own Choice: Circles and Squares		Pelvic Swing	Shoulder Stand (2)	
3	Sudden breath	2	Foot movements	1.4.2	Shoulder Stand (2)	Own Choice: Clock Face		Triangle	Shoulder Stand variations	
4	Sudden breath	2	Fingers on eyes; lips; forehead	Abdominal 1.4.2	Shoulder Stand variations	Breathing – Seated: Alternate nostrils		Half moon	Camel	
5	Sit and move feet	Salute 1–4	Fingers on eyes; lips; forehead	Abdominal 1.4.2	Camel	Own Choice: Self-awareness		Rishi	Fencer (1)	
6	Sit and move feet	Salute 1–6	1 → 8 → 1 1 → 4 → 1		Fencer (1)	Seated: Candle		Powerful Child	Fencer (2) variation	Discussion of progress
7	Standing breath	Salute 7–12	1 → 8 → 1 1 → 4 → 1		Fencer (2) variations	Seated: Candle		Knees in eyes	Standing twists	
8	Droop and Arch	Salute 1–12	Instant		Standing twists	Own Choice: Yoga Way of Life (5)		Balance – knees	Supine twists (1)	
9	Leg side raise	Salute 1–12	Instant		Supine twists (1)	Own Choice: Yoga Way of Life (6)		Balance – legs	Supine twists (2)	
10	Standing breath	3	Arms move	Arms and breath	Supine twists (2)	Own Choice: Yoga Way of Life (7)		Stand and sit	Prone twist	
11	Arm Swings	3	Arms move	Arms and breath	Prone twist	Own Choice: Yoga Way of Life (8)		Revision	Spine twist (1)	
12	Sudden breath	3	Revision	Revision	Revision	Revision		Revision	Revision	Suggestions: next term?

Diagram 7 A year's work in Yoga: (c) Summer

Weeks	*Limbering exercise*	*Routine (see text)*	*Relaxation*	*Breathing*	*Posture revision*	*Mental work and meditation*	BREAK	*'Quickies' (see text)*	*New posture*	*Free time, discussion*
1	Standing Breath	Salute to the Sun 1–6	Corpse	On all fours Abdominal	Spine Twist	Own Choice: Light		Squat and kneel; Cobra twist	Locust (1)	
2	Standing Breath	Salute 7–12	Corpse	On all fours Abdominal	Locust (1)	Own Choice: Sound		Cat and mod.; Head-stand	Locust (2)	
3	Forward Droop	Salute 1–12	Corpse	Bellows	Locust (2)	Own Choice: Warmth		Half Crab; Crab	Boat	
4	Backward Arch	1	Corpse	Bellows	Boat	Own Choice: Gita Reading (1)		Alternate Arm–Leg Head Flop	Swan	
5	Side leg Raise	1	Prone	Kneel; Expand	Swan	Own Choice: Gita Reading (2)		Pelvic swing; Triangle	Head of Cow	
6	Side leg Raise	2	Prone	Kneel; Expand	Head of Cow	Own Choice: Yoga View of Life (9)		Half Moon; Rishi	Tree	
7	Arm Swing	2	Own Choice	Own Choice	Tree	Own Choice: 8 Limbs		Balances	Eagle	Discuss next year
8	Sit: Move knees	3	Own Choice	Own Choice	Eagle	Own Choice: Yoga View of Life (10)		Revision	Chest Stretch	Discuss next year
9	Revision	3	Own Choice	Own Choice	Revision	Revision		Revision	Revision	Discuss next year
10	Revision	3	Own Choice	Own Choice	Revision	Revision		Revision	Revision	Discuss next year

(iii) Note the order of events: limbering exercises, routines, relaxation, breathing, postures, meditation, 'quickies', postures and free time. Experience suggests this as giving variety and presenting the right activity at the right time.

(iv) Some of the names of movements and postures may be unfamiliar. In fact there may be a growing tendency to use different names in different areas. A check list at the end of this chapter will clarify this. (See Diagram 12.)

(v) Routines: a routine is a carefully constructed sequence giving just the right amount of gentle exercise to the whole body, with optional breathing sequences, to prepare the class for relaxation and breathing. Routines 1 and 2 are the author's own 'inventions' (Diagrams 8 and 9); Routine 3 is the four Mudras (Diagram 10), performed in various positions – standing, sitting, kneeling, squatting, or supine; and Routine 4 is the Salute to the Sun (Diagram 11).

Note: I am avoiding Sanskrit titles, not because of any prejudice, but because there are many who find themselves taking classes and have no good reason for learning them.

(vi) 'Quickies': these are small, often curious, and always engaging movements and postures that follow naturally after a break, and usually introduce an atmosphere of informality. Once again, the titles may be unfamiliar but will be clarified in a summary list at the end.

(vii) Alternate arm and leg stretch is performed in the all fours position. Each arm and leg in turn is extended horizontally from the shoulder or hip and, as a variation, an arm and leg together may be extended: left with right, or two lefts (and two rights).

(viii) Relaxation and breathing 1 → 8 → 1, 1 → 4 → 1 consists of making the body progressively rigid on a count up to eight (or four), later adding a breath, and relaxing the body to a count down from eight (or four), releasing the breath.

(ix) The 'Powerful Child' is a more dynamic form of the Child Posture: what many teachers call the Yoga Mudra (see the list of postures at the end of this chapter).

(x) Instant relaxation and breathing is like (viii) above, but instantly, to command. This facility is clearly useful as a growing natural ability for moments of unexpected tension.

Diagram 8 Routine 1

Diagram 9 Routine 2

Diagram 10 Routine 3 The four Mudras

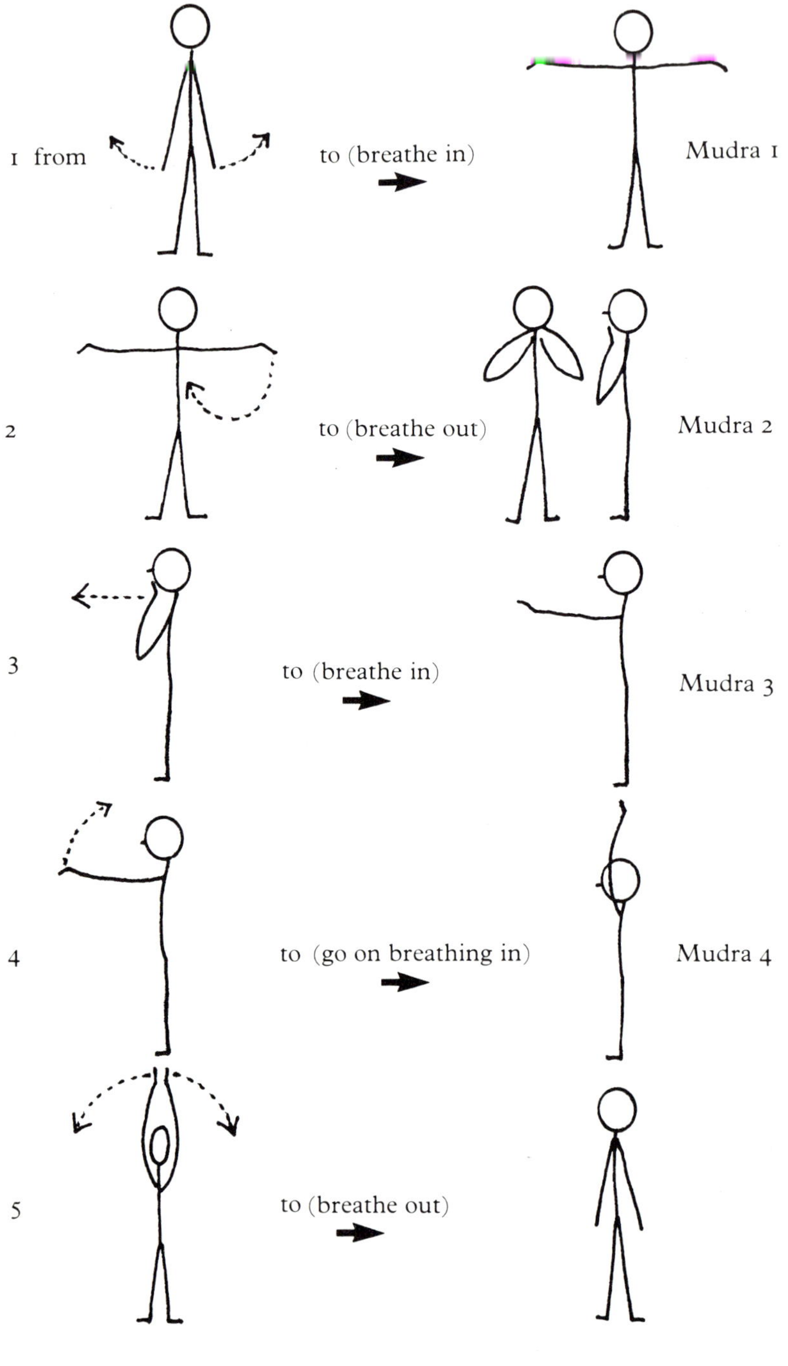

Diagram 11 Routine 4 Surya Namaskar: Salute to the Sun

(xi) Sit: bend knees. Sitting with knees bent, hands on the floor giving general support. Bend whole leg and knee unit over to the left. Keep legs together, and contemplate the soles of the feet. Go left, right, two or three times.

At the end of the third term, as we have mentioned in a previous chapter, it will be clear that many will want to continue. It would be as well to present the case for two kinds of class for these people:

(a) A class for experienced pupils who really just want to go over the same ground again.

(b) A class for pupils who are willing to commit themselves to two further years, probably with the same teacher.

For these last, a three-year course must be planned, or rather, the second and third years of such a course.

In the second year there will be new material in the following areas: postures, breathing and relaxation techniques and meditation; combining breathing and movement; holding postures with mental concentration; a well-defined resolution to attempt Yoga habits.

In the third year the work will have to be individual. The whole session, apart from the beginning (perhaps the Salute, or some agreed sequences), and the end (a group meditation, or an Om chant) will comprise free time: the leader (not a teacher now) dealing with individuals as persons, usually with some considerable knowledge of them as persons, and of their backgrounds. Probably the third year group (and other interested persons) will want to go away for residential weekends. Some may begin to think about taking a teachers' course, and will be in a good position to do so after a three-year intensive course such as we have described.

Day Seminars

Where planning is concerned, this is quite a simple matter:

1. Choose your venue, bearing in mind locality, clientele, costs and accommodation. Seek LEA subsidies, but don't depend upon them.
2. Establish your needs with the Centre.
3. Publicize well, months in advance if possible.
4. Decide on the programme, usually the following:

10.30	*Coffee*
11.00 – 1.00	*First session: Introduction – relaxation – breathing – meditation.*
1.00 – 2.00	*Light lunch.*
2.00 – 3.00	*Second session: Background – philosophy – discussion.*
3.00 – 3.30	*Tea (a cup of tea and a biscuit).*
3.30 – 5.00	*Final session: Relaxation – postures – meditation – discussion.*

These are only the briefest of introductory notes. This is not the place for details: in any case, they will depend very much on circumstances. We must not confuse pre-planning with management, which will feature in the next chapter, and is the way you ensure the successful completion of your plans.

Weekend Courses

Experience is the key. There is enough to be said to fill a book itself, but we must keep to essentials here.

Needless to say, you will wish to settle for a congenial venue, and probably return there regularly. Check the economics carefully, and delegate money matters to a colleague. Have visiting speakers to lend variety. Establish real social links and encourage informality.

Timetable – try the following:

Friday	
7 pm	*Arrive – register – supper.*
8.30 pm	*Introductions – general survey – meditation.*
Saturday	
9 am	*Gentle breathing and relaxation.*
11 am	*Routines and postures.*
2 pm	*Visiting speaker.*
4 pm	*Meditation.*
8 pm	*Informal evening: films, slides about India.*
Sunday	
9 am	*Gentle breathing and posture routines.*
11 am	*Visiting speaker.*
2 pm	*Open forum and final meditation.*

Courses of this kind are excellent as regular, perhaps annual, gatherings of teachers. Ideally, the teachers in each area should form an Association, which adopts a Centre, and meets residentially at least once, preferably twice in each year, to exchange experience, perfect their own Yoga, and meet experts not only in Yoga, but in related fields.

Diagram 12 A check list of common postures

Arm and leg raise

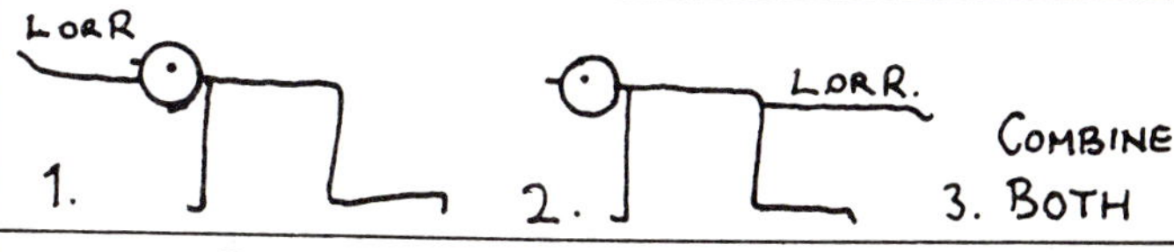

Backward arch

Back stretch

Bow

Boat

Camel

or

Cat

Chest stretch

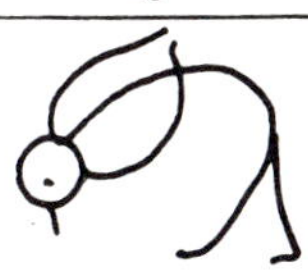

Clockface

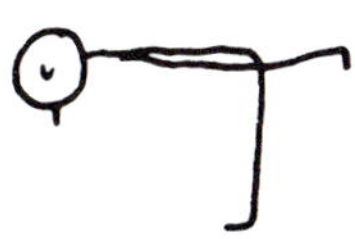

Child

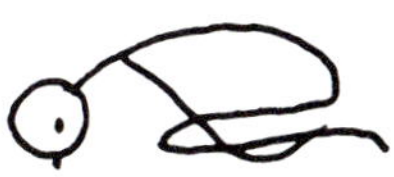

Powerful Child

Cobra

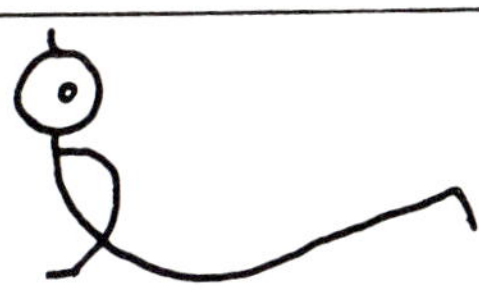

Cobra Twist

Crab	 Armless Cobra 
Dancer	 Dancer king 
Fencer	  Variations 
Half moon	 Triangle (Rishi's) 
Head of a cow	 Head to knee 
Hip twist	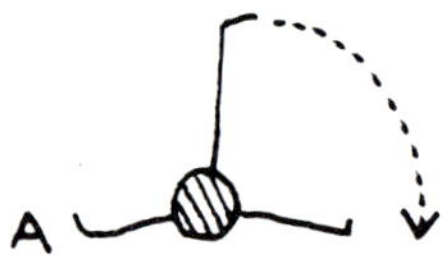 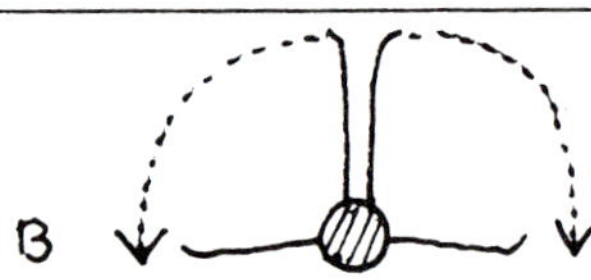
Knee balance	 Leg balance 
Knees in eyes	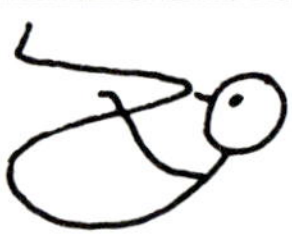 Nose on knees 
Leg stretch	  OR 
Locust	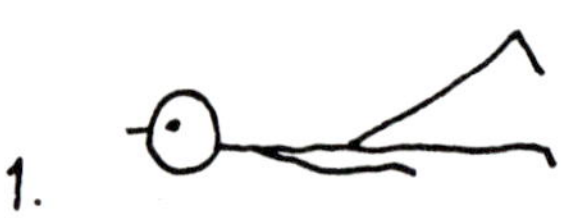 

Lotus

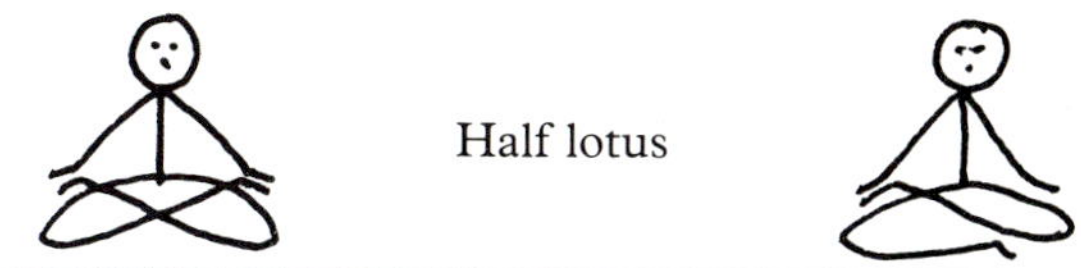

Plough

Shoulder stand

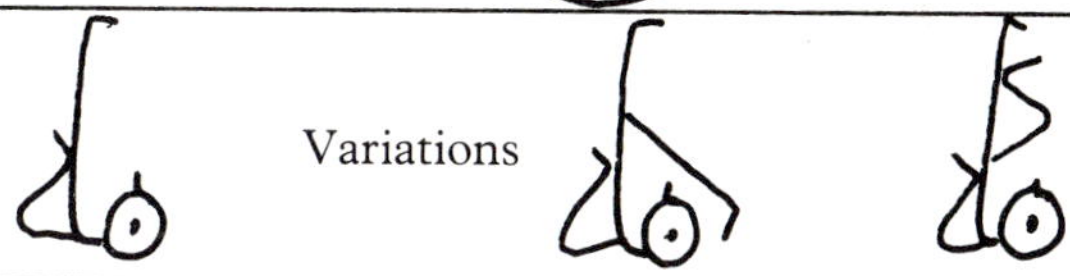

Twists

Swan

Tree

Shoulder pull

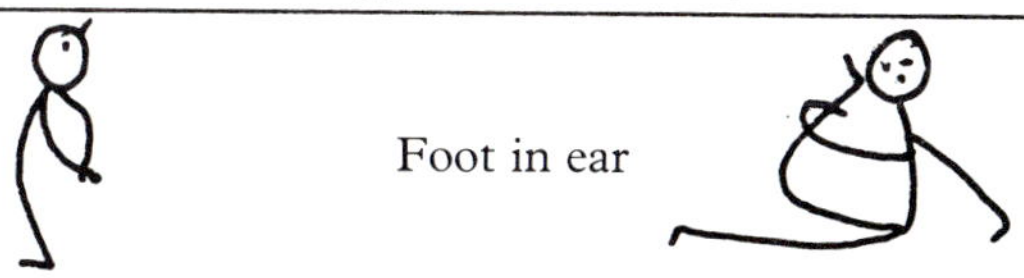

Heel swing

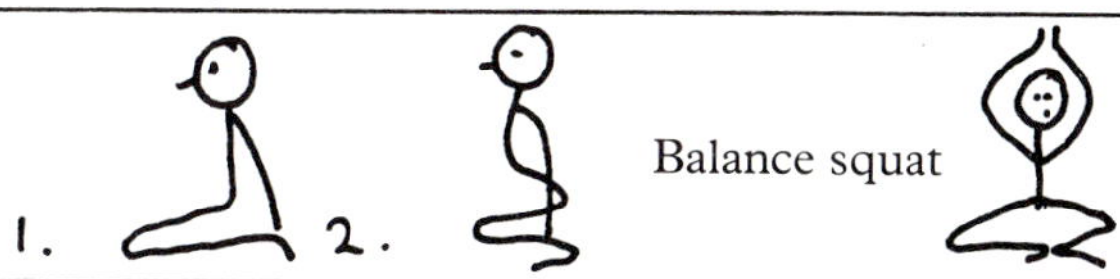

Pagoda feet

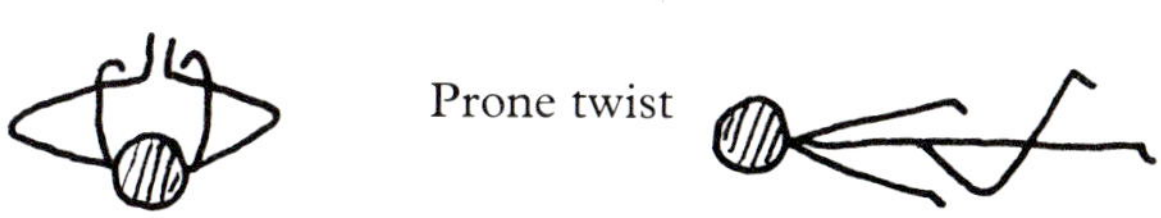

Pointer

6: Class Management

Class management is the practical business of taking a group successfully through its series of sessions. This must be done in such a way that the following standards are achieved:

– the class is satisfied; the teacher is satisfied; a good standard of Yoga has been sustained; no one has any ill-effects; there have been no accidents; no one has been offended; the teacher is not over-tired; those responsible for the premises are satisfied; the room is left in good order; the sessions relate to those that have gone before and those that are to follow; financial, administrative and lost property matters are properly dealt with.

We shall take these matters under three headings:

1. Management
2. Safety
3. Ethics

These areas of consideration overlap, of course, but it is easier to take them in turn.

1. *Management*

Three objectives here:

(a) Get the class into the room, regularly; minimise progressive drop out; welcome latecomers and late-joiners.

(b) Keep the class happy, but hard at work; give them 'their money's worth'; send them home rested but aware that they have 'worked themselves out'.

(c) Please all concerned; class, demonstrator, officers at the centre, caretaker.

They are not difficult objectives, and we are not suggesting that there is such a thing as a model Yoga teacher, or a standard of uniformity which we should aim at. But a number of suggestions, many of them born of bitter experience, may be of interest. As in so many fields of education, the teacher who is good at class management can get by with considerably less than first-class expertise, but the expert, be he ever so intellectual, supple or mystical, will get nowhere with a class unless he learns class management.

(i) The class arrives, usually in twos and threes. Establish the habit of their taking up a seated posture and performing a relaxing movement or two until the session begins. This should be no later than five minutes after the advertised starting time.

(ii) Mark the beginning of the session with a greeting, a casual remark or two, and start straight into the first activity: establish the relationship of teacher and taught from the very start.

(iii) Partially ignore latecomers. Make visual signals indicating vacant spaces, with a smile, but don't interrupt the flow of the session, or draw the class's attention to the interruption.

(iv) Most of those present will want, in the best sense, to 'vegetate': they want to be led. So lead: 'talk through' the exercises, giving general advice, without making reference to individuals. If necessary, stop the class, and indicate common faults. A touch of humour here and there will set many timid minds at rest. Try not to be a distant idol, nor yet a casual friend.

(v) Voice control is important: be firm but persuasive. Careful use of the voice can lead to a class hanging on every word. When this happens the teacher is in a very privileged position. He can bring deep relaxation very quickly to nervously taut emotions. But those not endowed with 'voice' need not lose heart: what is less successful orally will usually be more than made up for by the visual element.

(vi) Praise everybody, especially at the end of a group movement. Never criticise individuals. If a fault appears that needs immediate correction, stop, point out a 'common fault' and start again.

(vii) What about the business of 'demonstrators'? They certainly have their uses, particularly in showing new postures, breathing techniques, and revision, or variations of old postures. But make the class watch: stand behind the demonstrator and describe what is happening. Indicate the aspects of the movement or posture that matter most. Remember that in most postures the class cannot 'do' and watch at the same time, so there is little point in the demonstrator or teacher using valuable energy 'performing' when the class cannot see anything of what is happening! The chapters on detailed teaching method will assume the presence of a demonstrator, and a demonstrator is used in the accompanying photographs, so we shall return to this topic later.

(viii) Strangely enough, odd remarks slipped in now and then are often most clearly remembered, so take advantage of this. It becomes monotonous, not to say offensive, to introduce each posture in the same way every time. Try to be conversational; perhaps, now and then, a little autobiographical; and don't be afraid to admit your own weaknesses. ('I can't really do this one very well, but I'm sure you can . . . .')

(ix) The 'odd remark' system works admirably for meditation too, especially at the beginning. A class will be delighted to be told, after lying still, quietly breathing, and counting the seconds of their own breathing scheme, that they have just done their first meditation. In fact, if you tell them to think carefully about each movement they make, they will get into a meditative mood for the whole evening. In many ways, it is wrong to distinguish activities too clearly.

(x) What about having a break? I suggest not, especially if the session is limited to ninety minutes. But there should be a short informal 'space for oddments'. If possible, the registers should be dealt with at this halfway point, because this is the time when most pupils will be present. This is also the time when announcements can be made, books recommended, and private queries invited. There are lots of good reasons for *not* having time for queries and other matters at the end of the session. It may be that another class is waiting, or you may have to go elsewhere, or the caretaker is waiting to lock up. Very often such discussions (or 'consultations') can take place during 'free time' – a good reason for introducing it.

(xi) Questions from the class during the session – actually during working time – should be taken up, and if possible thrown open for discussion. Informal casting about of ideas is often the way proper discussions begin.

(xii) If anyone is in difficulties then a visual signal with the eyes or hand to 'sit this one out' is the best way. You will have made it clear more than once that the idea is to select what is enjoyable, beneficial and satisfying, and to put aside the unsuitable, impossible and uncongenial.

(xiii) Sometimes there will be the unexpected: so here is a short list of Do's and Don't's:

- Pupil with coughing spasm: have glass of water handy. Pupil should sit forward. You need not speak: class will appreciate your kind thought and find it relaxing.
- Pupil clearly *doesn't like* postures: wander over, and suggest that he relaxes quietly. Speak to him at break and discuss his future attendance.
- Pupil clearly *doesn't like* meditation: suggest that he sits at the back and continues with quiet postures. Discuss his future attendance.
- No heating: take a one-hour busy session of routines and breathing, and depart to home fires burning.

(xiii) Recommending literature each week is a good idea: likewise magazines, records, and the occasional stock-in-trade of the avid Yogi: joss-sticks, mandalas, sandalwood cones.

(xiv) Close the class properly: bid them farewell and say you look forward to the next meeting. Then turn your attention to yourself: remember to conserve your own energies.

2. *Safety*

What can go wrong? Many things: physical, mental, emotional. A few rules will ensure that the teacher has not been negligent. LEA teachers are covered by insurance, but this will not apply if they have not taken reasonable precautions. So try to have:

(i) A first aid box handy.

(ii) Knowledge of the best advice or immediate treatment for the one person in very many weeks who faints, for the much more common cramp, sudden headache, dizziness, or the frequently quite natural but somewhat disconcerting tears, usually during meditation.

(iii) Knowledge of the local doctor's telephone number.

(iv) Awareness of any qualified persons in the class.

(v) Knowledge of the human body and mind, which will constitute the best prevention of many emergencies. You will have noticed that many postures do not figure in the schemes (viz: Headstand, Peacock).

3. *Ethics*

Yoga is a personal affair, and the Yoga teacher is in a privileged position. Physically, mentally, emotionally and sometimes spiritually he has access to people in ways that are very rare in other fields. Very often one hears: 'Since I have been attending Mr. A's classes my life has been transformed. I am a happier, healthier person.' Teachers can sometimes discern that pupils are deriving a very deep personal benefit from their classes.

There are many good reasons for having a 'code of ethics', for the Yoga teacher's own protection.

A Yoga Teacher's Code of Ethics

1. A Yoga teacher should have, or seek, nationally or locally acceptable official qualifications, and the support of three reputable referees.
2. He (or she) should be a member of an Association. (Such an Association is the Wheel of Yoga.)
3. Any physical contact with pupils, or demonstrators, during the course of a public class, should be clearly consistent with the work in hand, and seen to be so. Absence of any affectation or mannerism will ensure against misinterpretation.
4. He must be aware of any influence he may have on his pupils beyond his Yoga teaching, e.g. a quasi-hypnotic effect during relaxation, or the encouragement of an emotional dependence upon him on the part of some pupils. This influence cannot be ruled out, but, once recognised, must be closely controlled.

5. Any personal admissions made to him during a private interview are, by definition, confidential.
6. He will not discuss the relative merits of his colleagues with anyone. If a difficult situation arises, it will be proper and appropriate to invite the intervention of the Provincial Member of the Wheel of Yoga, or the appropriate LEA Adviser.
7. Before undertaking private coaching, he should not only be aware of, and undertake, the standards of this Code, but should make it clear that the private pupil is in attendance at his own wish, and at his own risk. If there is any hint of doubt, the pupil should be advised to bring a companion.
8. No work with children should be undertaken without there being a clear opportunity for parents to know that it is happening, to visit the group, and to withdraw their children if they wish.
9. The teacher should dress in a manner consistent with the nature and purpose of Yoga. Leotards and tights for women, or shirt and gymnastic trousers for men, are most suitable. Some pupils will find a man teacher dressed only in shorts embarrassing to watch.
10. There is great value in having the Yoga class visited, from time to time, by an Official of the LEA, or the Regional Representative of the Wheel of Yoga. It is possible for a group to become affiliated to the Wheel of Yoga.

Note to Chapters 7, 8, 9 and 10

The next four chapters deal with methods of teaching four aspects of Yoga in classroom situations. It is to these chapters that many will turn for immediate information about ways of presenting postures, teaching relaxation or breathing, or leading a meditation.

For this reason, and also because it makes for more spontaneous writing, and more engaging and vivid reading, these chapters have been set in typical but fictitious class situations. We shall imagine, for the greater part of the time, that we have the luxury of a good demonstrator. We must add, though, that any reasonably experienced pupil could demonstrate: it does not demand necessarily any great expertise, only the willingness to co-operate with the teacher, and be stared at! Several members might offer to be a demonstrator, on a rota system, or the teacher may be on friendly enough terms with his class to draw attention to what one person is doing.

Some Education Authorities will pay a demonstrator, and this is a good stepping-stone to becoming a Yoga teacher.

So in the next few chapters, please imagine that a class is in progress: the words are those of the teacher, except where the demonstrator or a class member contributes something to a short discussion, or asks a question.

Remember that demonstrators are there to reflect good teaching and bad practice, and a good teacher will often work a demonstrator hard for short periods, and then let him or her relax whilst the class is engaged in something else. Don't be afraid to manipulate the demonstrator: wholesome, friendly prods and grips on limbs, joints and body areas vital to good postures cannot cause offence, and are just what the class need, visually, to accompany the teacher's oral commentary.

The photographs referred to in these chapters will show something of the way in which a demonstrator can be used. Without one, the teacher will usually comment on his own postures: this is not impossible, but can sometimes be difficult, especially in inverted postures!

Note: The sequence: relaxation, breathing, postures and mind training, is quite arbitrary. How they are combined in the session is part of the teacher's planning (Chapter 5).

7: Teaching Relaxation

1. *Relaxation in the Corpse posture (a)*

Teacher: I'm going to ask Jane to show you one of the ways you can relax in the Corpse posture. Come as near as you like: those at the back can stand up.
(Jane takes up Corpse posture. She has a 7 ft. × 7 ft. platform, 12 ins. high and 7 ft. × 7 ft. mat. The class gathers on three sides, leaving the teacher freedom to move behind her.)
Teacher: Jane has started to relax already, beginning with her feet. Look: when I move her foot it falls back into position like a dead weight. Did you notice that the whole leg moved as well? Watch again: the other leg this time.
Now look at her hands. If I straighten her fingers they curl again, just a little. If I 'roll' her arm, the whole arm moves – right up to the shoulder, and then rolls back, and settles.

Now she's closing her eyes: closing the doors of vision. As far as she's concerned, we are not here! She's letting her head 'slump' slowly over to one side: that slump is an exciting and relaxing feeling. If I lift her head up, it feels very heavy, and it will fall again when I take my hand away. She will stop with her head in the normal position, so that there is no heavy feeling, either way.

Jane's going to lie there and relax whilst you return to your mats . . .
Lie down on your backs . . . .
Try to get all of yourself on the mat, especially your head. Let yourself get used to the idea of 'just lying there'. If you are feeling impatient or bored, then clearly you need Yoga! Think about what you are going to do: so simple, yet so absorbing – quite unlike anything else.

It's called the Corpse posture: you're going to let yourself die. Feel the mat under you solid but soft.
Voice: I'm not used to this: my head feels wrong, and the small of my back feels in mid-air.
Teacher: Have you got a coat or something to rest your head on? Bring a little cushion next week. Don't bother about your back, it's quite usual.
Will you all arrange your feet, with your heels close (they needn't touch) and your toes apart.
Press your toes – your feet – up together.
Let them fall apart.
Push your toes further down – towards the floor . . . .
Let them lift again.
Now leave them alone – that bit of you is 'dead'.
Slowly make fists with your hands: tighter . . . tighter . . . .
Relax the fists: uncurl your fingers – straighten your fingers.
Stretch your fingers back, and wide apart . . . .
Let your fingers curl again, slowly.
Now leave them alone – those bits of you are 'dead'.
Think about closing your eyes. You're going to do it like Jane did it: by slowly pulling down the shutters. Begin now: slowly close the doors of vision. Look inwardly – at yourself – busy with a pleasant occupation of relaxation. Now everyone's eyes are gently closed.
Think about your head – your mind: the source of the powers of sense and observation, of thinking, making decisions, feeling emotions.
Feel your head falling to one side, but control the fall at first.
Let the falling get stronger: lose control, *and . . . flop.*

Stay there.

Tension ebbs away; it's nice to have nothing to do, to be alone, just to lie there and do nothing: a chance to have a few minutes to yourself.
Bring your head slowly up: keep your eyes closed.
Feel your head up straight – but don't look!
Now leave it alone: that bit of you is 'dead' . . . .
Your body may not feel very relaxed: it takes a long time to learn.
It takes ages to teach your body to be quiet and still.

2. *Relaxation in the Corpse posture (b)*

Teacher : Come round the platform again . . . .
Jane has already let herself down into deep physical relaxation. I'm not going to check by moving her feet or her head: that would arouse a response, and spoil her feeling of rest.
What I want you to do is to watch her breathing . . . .
Notice lots of things (pre-arranged with Jane if possible):
1. She is breathing in through her nose and out through her mouth: not essential, but a good way to start.
2. The breathing is very gentle, but you can easily make it out.
3. Most of the breathing is in the tummy area: allowing the diaphragm inside to expand downward, and the lower lungs to fill with air.
4. Let's watch three or four cycles of breathing, and count to ourselves the number of seconds for each part: breathing in, holding the full breath, breathing out, staying empty.
Now back to your mats.
Go through the relaxing process I taught you before, but combine each movement with a breath. Try it with me:
Lie quietly for a moment and think what you're going to do.
Brace your feet together and breathe in: 1. 2. 3. 4. 5.
Hold the breath and the position.
Release the breath gradually, and ease away the tension on your feet: 5. 4. 3. 2. 1.
Part your toes wide and breathe in: 1. 2. 3. 4. 5.
This time, when I count '5 to 1' release your breath, and let your feet go quickly: 5 to 1!
In a moment you can do the same with your hands.
With your head movement, breathe in first, and let it move over as you breathe out. I'll explain first: you will breathe in as I count to 8. Then, as I count down from 8, move slowly from 8 to 4, and then drop down on '4 to 1'.
Try it now: Breathe in: 1. 2. 3. 4. 5. 6. 7. 8. Breathe out and move slowly: 8. 7. 6. 5. – now quickly 4 to 1!

3. *Relaxation in Corpse posture (c)*

Teacher : Watch Jane. Someone please describe what's happening.

Voice 1 : She's breathing in.
Voice 2 : And becoming rigid.
Voice 3 : Clenched fists, pointed feet, arched back.
Voice 4 : Contorted face.
Voice 1 : Now she's breathing out again.
Voice 5 : And all the tension is going.
Voice 2 : It was a bit frightening to watch the in breath.
Voice 4 : But the breathing out was super to watch.
Teacher : Watch again: Jane's going to do that in the time of 3 seconds in, and 2 seconds out. I warn you – it will probably be noisy!
(Jane does so: it *is* noisy!)
Voice : I couldn't do that.
Teacher : Away to the mats, and let's try!
First we'll breathe in and become rigid over a count of 8, and 8 again to relax and breathe out . . . .
Now we'll try it with 6 . . . (Rest).
Now try it with 4 . . . (Rest)
Lastly, 3 in, and 2 out! . . . (Rest).
We call this 'instant relaxation': rather like performing a yawn or sigh really properly! It can be very useful when you have very little time!

4. *Relaxation in the prone position*

Teacher : Notice that Jane is lying on her stomach, arms bent forward as a head-rest, and her feet arranged with toes together and heels apart. She's resting her cheek on her hands.
Voice : You can't move very much of your body in this position.
Teacher : No, but you can use your legs to great effect. In fact, this is a good position for leg work. Relaxation in many ways consists of actually concentrating hard on something quite small or simple, with the result that the rest of your body, mind, emotions and nervous system get forgotten, take a holiday – call it what you like! You can't see Jane's breathing movement very well, so I'll rest my hand on her back, and tap my finger in time to her breathing.

As she breathes in you'll start to notice that she does tiny movements with her legs: the left foot moves a few inches to the left; and back; the right moves: a little lift, a shift and a

1 Correct sitting position (*page 68*)

2 Abdominal breathing – full (*page 74*)

3 Abdominal breathing – empty (*page 74*)

4 The Cobra (*page 84*)

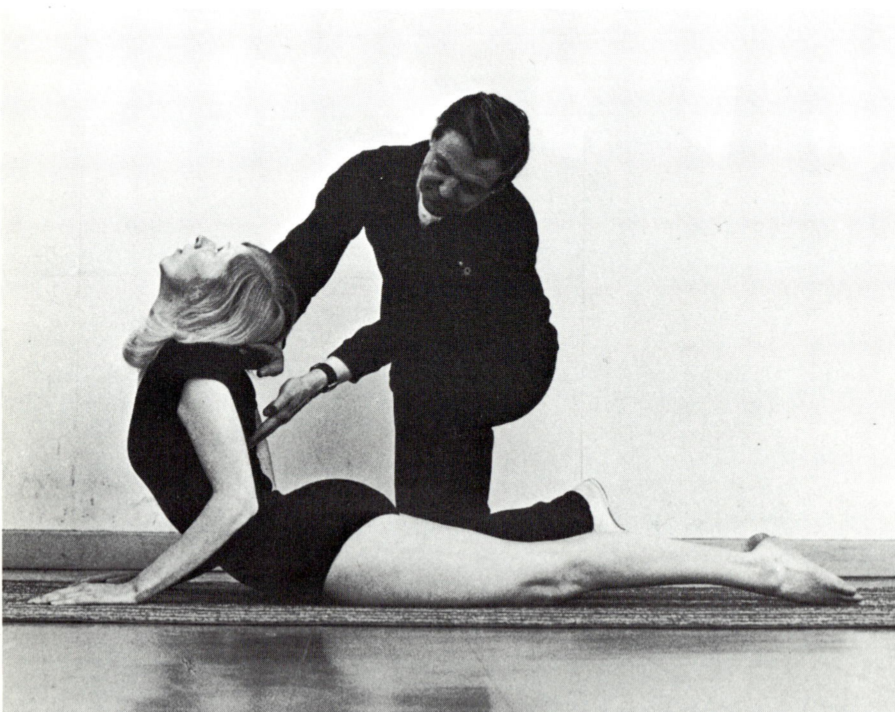

5 The Bow (*page 86*)

6 The Plough (*page 90*)

7 The Pose of Tranquillity (*page 91*)

8 The Backstretch (*page 91*)

9 The Camel
(*page 92*)

10 Simple Twist
(*page 94*)

11 Spine Twist
(*page 94*)

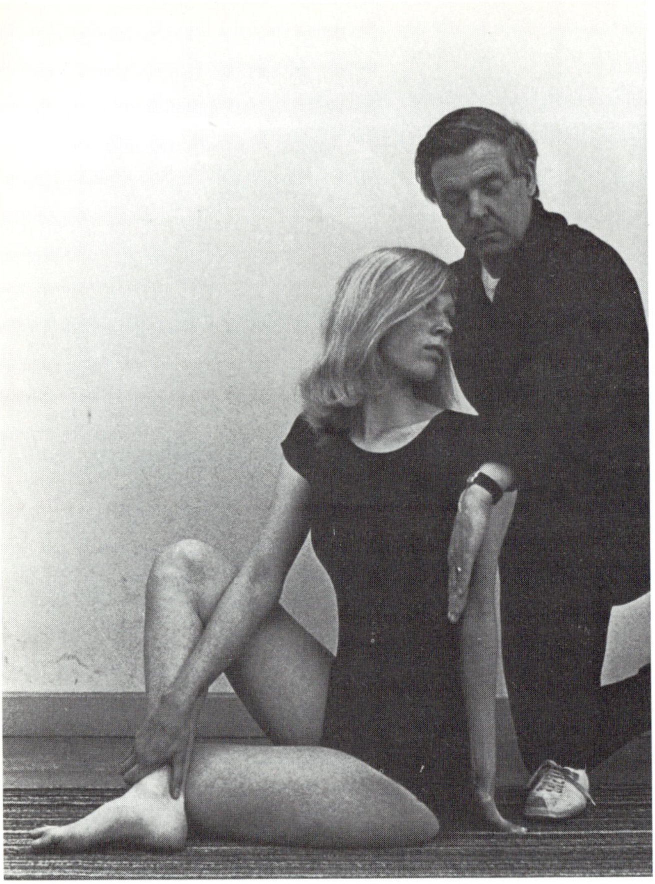

12 The Cat – up
(*page 96*)

13 The Cat – down (*page 96*)

14 The Locust (*page 97*)

15 The Child
(*page 97*)

16 Candle
Meditation
(*page 104*)

gentle drop; the two feet move apart . . . and together . . . and each in time to a breath: 'breathe in, move, stop moving, breathe out, rest, and then all over again. Lastly notice how she is starting to lift her left lower leg, from the knee, ever so slowly, with gentle regular breathing: and then down again. We'll not bother with the right leg – but watch now as she lifts both lower legs: no hurrying, no jerking – together – and back again.

Thank you, Jane.

Now it's your turn.

Get quite comfortable on your mats.

Start your steady breathing. It will be easier to breathe out in this position, especially if you are a bit stocky or thick set around the shoulders.

Take your own time, but follow this pattern: breathe in for 5, move a foot, settle again, breathe out for 5, and rest. Follow with the other foot, and then both feet.

Now try bending your legs: but mind, no jerks, no hurrying, and gentle breathing all the time.

If you want to try some advanced relaxation, try doing all these feet and leg movements again, but only in your *imagination.*

You've only just done them, so use your memory. Cast your mind back: recall what it felt like, and go through the motions in your mind – only do the correct breathing!

5. *Relaxation and the Four Mudras*

(The Four Mudras are shown in Diagram 10.)

Teacher : Relaxation lying down is the way to begin, but Yoga is relaxation all the way through, and you should approach each posture with relaxed attention. I shall be satisfied if you can tell me three things:

1. I find Yoga relaxing.
2. I find the Yoga exercises relaxing.
3. I enjoy the special Yoga-type relaxation that I do.

I shall be delighted if you come and tell me that really it's the other way round, and that you really are not sure where the relaxation stops and the exercises start!

Jane's going to be very patient tonight, and let you stare at her while she goes through the Four Mudras.

Jane : I enjoy doing the Mudras actually, so I don't mind at all doing them!

Teacher : You can do these standing up, kneeling, sitting or lying on your back. I want Jane to do them standing up, and I'll talk about them as she goes along.

You start simply standing naturally but well – and that's very hard! Let me show you:

Jane gets a good footing – plants herself on the floor, braces her legs tall, keeps her back naturally straight (most people have a natural little curve at the waist), tummy controlled but not tense, chest natural – certainly *not* stuck out! Her arms are tidily alongside her, hands resting on her thighs, neck and head upright, face alert but not strained.

How do you do all this *and* relax: well the truth is that you can't do it *unless* you *do* relax. Your mind must be right.

We're not into the first Mudra yet – but watch what happens now: she's breathing in, Yoga style: a great breath, building from the abdomen and filling through the diaphragm, and she's raising her arms till they stretch out from her shoulders, palms pointing down. The movement is relaxed, and so is the new position.

Mudra 1 Notice: she hasn't moved any other part of her body. (She's breathing gently while she waits for instructions!)

Voice : Must the arms be straight?

Teacher : I'll support Jane's left arm and she can rest the other one. Look at this left arm: there are one or two natural curves, but a centre line from shoulder to fingertip is horizontal, or parallel with the floor.

Right Jane: as you were.

Watch now: she brings her arms down and forward.

The hands approach each other, the palms come together. The fingertips come to rest roughly level with the lips but not touching them, the elbows lie rested near the body, the eyes take a long focus, and *the body is still*, apart from the ebb and flow of the breathing.

She has let her breath exhale during that movement, and she's now breathing gently till we move on again.

This is *Mudra 2*: one of the most sublime postures in the Art of Yoga. It has tremendous symbolism: greeting, contentment, readiness, obedience, modesty, wisdom. The personality 'comes to rest' and the experience is a marvellous base line for twenty-four hours of daily life.

Now she moves her hands forward: the palms part and turn, palms down, as the arms straighten. Once again, the arms are in line with the shoulders. If you are relaxed, your hands will be quiet and still – but don't worry if there is a little shaking. You may improve things when you have learned to breathe, and when you have learned to 'rest yourself into a posture'. Jane let her lungs fill full as she made the movement, and if she were doing this just for her own benefit she would go on breathing in into the next position. Put your arms down for a bit, Jane.

Voice: How long do you keep a position?

Jane: It varies with me: it depends on whether I'm tired or wide awake, and whether I want stimulation or relaxation.

Teacher: The paradox is that you can relax better if your mind is more alert. Relaxing is quite a precise art.

Now Jane, let's have your arms back up in front. Stay still for a moment – let the class have a good look at *Mudra 3*.

Watch now as Jane goes into the last position: this is the most important movement, because it involves more of the body than the others. It's only the arms that make a distinct movement, but watch what happens: as she lifts her arms, she keeps her head quite still, her eyes fixed fair and square on her 'point of focus', but there's a noticeable movement here, in the shoulders: both have lifted considerably; there's an expansion of the diaphragm (the rib-cage, actually), and a tightening of the muscles in the abdomen. Remember that, normally, she would be taking the second part of a long in-breath, so there is considerable tension (I don't mean strain). Notice that the fingers are pointing up, and the elbows are near the ears: many of you will not manage this!

So there we are: *Mudra 4*. The body is stretched, but not strained: it is a relaxed posture, but not a sloppy one.

She will take a breath now and return to the beginning by letting her arms slowly down, to the side, in a wide half-circle.

Sit down Jane, thank you.

You can do the movements sitting down, kneeling, squatting

or lying. Let's try it kneeling – I mean kneeling 'up' – on your knees – not 'down' on your heels.

Just try them at your own speed:

Get a steady kneeling posture first . . . . Don't bother with special breathing . . . . Arms by your sides . . . .

Now move to Mudra 1: arms rising to a line level with your shoulders. Look straight ahead.

Bring your hands together in front of you, like a prayer position: fingers near your lips. *Mudra 2.*

Extend your arms in front of you. Keep looking straight ahead. *Mudra 3.*

Keep your head still, and lift your arms up beside your ears: point your fingers. *Mudra 4.*

Bring your arms down the long way – a big, slow half circle. Did your notice that *Mudra 4* is quite difficult in the kneeling position?

Voice: My back's killing me!

Voices: And mine . . . and mine!

Well: it's only the first time, and I think you were trying too hard! You haven't really learned to 'relax into a posture!' We'll try it once more, all together, lying in the Corpse posture – down you go! . . .

6. *Relaxation in seated positions* (see Figure 1)

Teacher: It seems odd, but for all the complex postures and movements that we do, the position which comes to mind when you think of an Indian mystic deep in relaxed meditation, is that of a man (or a woman), just 'sitting' . . . just 'sitting' . · . . He probably has his legs crossed, or laid side by side, or in what we call the half-lotus, or full lotus posture . . . .

The way to a perfect seated position for relaxation is long and not always easy. That is because we have become accustomed to chairs – chairs of many kinds – most of them quite unsuitable.

Try sitting in a crosslegged position: Jane will help – only Jane will sit sideways so that I can point out the vital details of the correct position.

You can see it best if she starts by sitting badly! Notice the sloppy spine, the drooping head, the aimless arms and the angular knees. Consider all the points of tension, the potential points of discomfort and pain:

here: at the base of the spine
here: at the neck
here: in the shoulders, the elbows and the wrists
here: in the hips, knees and ankles.

Now watch a transformation:

1. A straight back: the spine 'stands up' by itself, on the pelvis, and carries the neck and the head, fair and square. There is no strain caused by leaning forward or back, or to one side or the other.
2. The arms are straight (not stretched), and rest on the knees.
3. The legs are lying quite flat; there is no strain: they are resting just where the hip joints will let them.
4. The head is erect, and the expression bright and alert.

This position embodies some of the basic principles of relaxation: poise, balance and contemplation. Relaxation is quite an alert, tidy, even 'smart and neat' experience. The feeling that everything about you: physically, mentally, emotionally, is 'just right'. You will probably want to feel convinced that you 'look right' as well. Clearly, if you strain, even in this position, you will start to ache, and you won't know whether you are straining until you do start to ache! In any case, it's unusual for you, something new, and will take some getting used to! Try one or two alternative leg positions – Jane will show you:

1. The legs are folded alongside each other: this avoids one ankle resting on the other.
2. Half lotus, one foot resting on the other thigh.
3. Full lotus: the feet both resting on the thighs.

Use these if you find them possible and helpful.

In this position, breathe naturally and deeply for 3 or 4 cycles, and rest for 3 or 4. Then repeat.

Jane's going to please herself what she does now.

Go to your mats, and we'll do this together, do what I say, when I say it (as far as you can, that is!).

Sit in a sloppy crosslegged position.

Come on – bent back, hang-dog head, arms all elbows and

wrists, shoulders hunched, looking at the floor, with your knees in your eyes nearly!

Now begin to change your position – wait! not too quickly: think about every inch of this movement:

1. Back starting to straighten, from the base of the spine.
2. Feel each bone coming into line.
3. Shoulders naturally erect: chest natural – not expanded, not restrained: tummy controlled, but not strained.
4. Neck feeling taller.
5. Head 'in the air' – high and attentive.
6. Eyes gently focused on a point at natural eye-level.
7. Face calm: breathing regular, conscious, but not exaggerated.
8. Arms extended, but not pulling shoulders out of shape.
9. Hands open: fingers straight.
10. Knees wide and low (it will take a long time for them to loosen – be patient over this).
11. Now sit still.
12. And 'listen to your own breathing'.

Alright: that's good for a first attempt – now . . . *flop*! – back to the beginning.

Voices : That wasn't very relaxing. – Gosh: that's sheer hard work. – I'll never get to work in the morning. – I'm sure my legs will fall right off. – When's coffee?

Teacher : How nice to hear you all enjoying yourselves! We'll try it again next week!

8: Teaching Breathing

1. *How breathing works*

Teacher : We breathe all the time. Most of the breathing that we do is unconscious, and badly done.

In Yoga session too we breathe all the time, and most of the breathing we do is unconscious. But it should be improved breathing. In relaxation, postures and meditation we do a great deal of thoughtful, self-conscious breathing of various kinds.

When we are specially concerned with breathing, there are things we must know about, and things we must do, to improve our breathing. We must concentrate entirely on the way we breathe: using our eyes, hands, ears, lips, our imagination and our sensations, to learn how to breathe in the best way we can. We are all different in health, physique, and breathing capacity, but we must each find our potential, and extend it.

How does breathing work?

All you need to know is that when you breathe in, you fill your lungs with air, and when you breathe out you empty your lungs, ready for the next breath.

Remember all the time that everything depends on your diaphragm and on the various cavities in your body near your lungs.

Your diaphragm is a kind of skin which supports your lungs. In Yoga you learn how to control your diaphragm.

The cavities can be expanded, to allow the lungs to expand as well. The whole effect is to help the lungs to fill to capacity, stay full and allow the air to be converted into energy in the blood, and then empty completely, ready for the next breath.

Breathing is basic to Yoga: I'll tell you how as we go along. Let's make a start. Stand up please: stand well, but easily and without strain. Let your arms hang loosely by your side.
Breathe gently and easily – in through your nose, out through your mouth.
Now start to breathe more powerfully. Feel the air rushing through your nose; retain your breath for a moment; and release the air again, through your mouth. Squeeze all the air out.
Do six breaths just like that, whilst I tap out seconds for you. Time yourselves. Find out what your normal, good breathing time is: how many seconds do you need for a complete cycle of breathing?
(Tap – tap – tap . . . at intervals of one second, for about two minutes.)

2. *Improving normal breathing*

To improve your normal, everyday breathing, you only need to know what happens when you breathe. Then you can convert your unconscious, often lazy breathing, into something dynamic, stimulating and satisfying. Sit comfortably and watch me. I don't mind being stared at – that's what I'm paid for!
Notice what I'm doing now: I'm pushing my tummy out, and pulling it in – just as a muscle exercise – I'm not breathing in time to the movements: if I did I couldn't go on talking! And just to prove it I'll lay my hands across my tummy.
In the normal position the fingers just touch; in the full position they are far apart; in the empty position they overlap.
Now it's your turn! Stand up and stand well: arms at your side.
Push your tummy out . . . pull it in . . . push out . . . pull in . . . .
Go on doing it – and have a look at what's happening: watch your tummy 'pumping away'.
Now let the movement subside . . . .
Lay your hands on your tummy, as I did: I'll do it again.
Finger-tips touch at the normal position.

Push out: push your hands apart.
Squeeze in and bring your hands together . . . will they overlap?
Try again: when you push out, use your tummy muscles to push against your hands. When you squeeze in, bear down with your hands.
Now start to breathe in time with your hands. Let's do it together: make lots of noise – you'll have to if you're doing it properly . . . .
Push. 2. 3. 4. 5. 6.
Squeeze. 2. 3. 4. 5. 6.
(Repeat 4 times.)
Now rest. Sit down if you wish. Watch me again.
That pushing and pulling with your tummy has the effect of lifting and lowering your diaphragm, and that helps to fill the lowest parts of your lungs.
To fill the middle section of your lungs better, you need a rib-expansion movement.
This is not so easy, so I'll use my hands straight away. I place them around my lowest ribs. Once again, in the normal position, fingers just touch. When I expand my ribs – sideways this time – the fingers part company, and when I squeeze the ribs together, the fingers overlap.
Notice again: it's a muscular movement, and I'm doing it without altering my breathing.
Try it: place your hands as I have. I'll do it again.
Start your movements – now you'll find this harder, because there's less movement. And some of you will have more powerful muscles than others. Remember: it's not how much movement you make, but making a real movement, however small, and making it well, that matters.
Try breathing as well:
Push. 2. 3. 4. 5. 6.
Squeeze. 2. 3. 4. 5. 6.
(Repeat 4 times.)

These two movements are the major elements in normal breathing. Practice them whenever you have the chance: as often as you like!

3. *Yoga breathing: (a) with the abdomen* (see Figures 2 and 3)

Come round the platform and watch Jane: she's lying in the Corpse posture, and she's quite used to being stared at. Jane's going to do Yoga breathing with her abdomen. Watch carefully: I'll use my hand to indicate what's happening.

She's starting to breathe in: the abdomen expands upwards, slowly but steadily. When fully expanded, the highest point is just below the navel. Now the abdomen relaxes, and squeezes down into a saucer shape – lowest point: just above the navel.

Watch the movement again and notice, at the end, that it isn't just a saucer, but there's a real hollow just under the ribs, where the diaphragm has been lifted, from inside, to squeeze the lungs empty.

Notice: only the abdomen is moving. The rest of the body is still and at rest. Notice the speed of the movement. We'll do a count on the next two cycles:

Breathing in: 1 . . . 8
Holding the breath full: 1 . . . 16
Releasing the breath: 1 . . . 8
Empty: 1 . . . 8

(Twice, with a few shallow breaths in between.)

That's 40 seconds for the whole cycle.

With some training, and in spite of being slim, Jane could probably increase that to 60 seconds from time to time: one breath per minute. She would have to take some shallow breaths between the big ones.

Come on – it's your turn now. You won't be able to see Jane, so there's no point in her doing it with you. She can do what she likes.

4. *Yoga breathing: (b) with the rib-cage*

Watch Jane again.

This time, as she breathes, she expands her ribs from side to side, and brings them together as she breathes out. But this is a Yoga type of breathing, so she concentrates on the rib cage, and the abdomen is still.

Jane: It's jolly hard, and I'm not very good at it.

Voices : That's quite all right, it makes us feel better!
Teacher : Another way that Yoga applies is that you think of breathing as the flow of energy, or the awakening of deeper personality, or the taking in of joy, and the releasing of tension. Releasing breath from the ribs (as it were) whilst keeping the tummy still is very hard, but let's all try.
Lie on your mats in the Corpse posture.
Take one minute to relax: count up to sixty slowly.
Now: place one hand on your tummy, to make sure it doesn't move, and the other on the side of your rib cage. Now think about 'breathing with your ribs'. Try gently and patiently until you get the idea . . . .
Perform some gentle, normal breaths every now and then.
Now try to do three good 'rib-breaths' in a row.
Energy flowing in: keep it inside you for a moment.
Tension flowing out: squeeze out every little bit!
Try again: watch yourselves . . . listen to your own breathing.

5. *Yoga breathing : (c) with the shoulders*

Sit and face me. Do what I do.
I'm sitting with my hands on my knees, legs out in front of me.
Now I'm lifting one of my shoulders. It doesn't matter which one. It lowers back to normal.
Now I lower it further. Quite a big movement there.
Try with the other shoulder: up . . . normal . . . down.
Now both shoulders: up . . . keep up there . . . nearly by your ears! . . . normal . . . down . . . .
Now raise your arms up – like me – towards the ceiling.
Now push one hand up higher than the other: keep it there.
Now push the other hand right past it! Come on! Have a real stretch!
Now keep your shoulders right up high . . . bring your arms slowly down – the long way, and,
Lower your shoulders!
Voices : Phew! – That was an enormous stretch! – I'll never be the same again!
Teacher : Well, the idea was to show you that you can make a lot of movement in your shoulders, and that movement releases cavities so that the upper part of your lungs can

receive air. Now watch Jane. She's lying in the Corpse posture, but her arms are behind her – lying along the platform. Her fingers are just touching a piece of wood, about two feet long (it could be a book, or two books). Now, as she breathes in, she stretches back with her arms, touches the wood, and pushes it about an inch away from her. As she breathes out her arms relax. And she does it all again, pushing the wood a little bit further. As this is a Yoga breath, the abdomen and rib-cage are still. Actually, they can't move very much, because of the arm position. Now it's your turn! When you've done the movement with your arms behind you, try it with your arms by your sides.

6. *Yoga breathing: the whole breath*

Watch Jane again: she's going to do a whole Yoga breath, in the Corpse posture.

While she relaxes, let me explain that a whole Yoga breath is like filling a glass with water: from the base to the brim, and emptying it again: from the brim to the base. Now Jane's ready to start.

First she slowly fills her abdomen.

Then she expands her ribs.

Lastly she fills her shoulder cavities and her upper chest – just under her chin. Now she starts to breathe out.

First she lets her upper chest recede – nothing else moves.

Then she relaxes her ribs – abdomen still full.

Lastly the abdomen contracts. And the next cycle begins.

The cycle can take a long time, or a little, as you please. But people say that when they've really learned how to breathe like this it's very hard to breathe quickly, and not very satisfying either. The hardest part is to keep your tummy up when your chest is going down! It's really an exercise in concentration, and that's good Yoga too.

You can move your arms up and over as you go along, if you like, and reach back like she did just now: or just keep them by your side and fill the shoulder cavities without actually moving your arms.

So lie on your mats please.

One hand on your tummy: the other on your ribs.

Just experiment on your own: fill your tummy (that's how it seems, anyhow); then add the rib expansion; finish off with your upper chest raising.

Breathe out the other way: upper chest recedes, ribs relax, and tummy squeezes . . . .

It doesn't matter if it doesn't go right: you may not get it right for a long time yet. But if you try *properly*: that is, try *patiently*, every breath will still be a good one.

Let's try it together. Don't worry if it goes wrong: just try to keep 'with the beat'. I'll call in groups of five, and we'll do it twice.

Prepare to breathe in:
Fill your abdomen. 3. 4. 5.
Expand your ribs. 3. 4. 5.
Lift your chest. 3. 4. 5.
Still.
Lower your chest. 3. 2. 1.
Relax your ribs. 3. 2. 1.
Squeeze your tummy. 3. 2. 1.
(Do this twice.)

Use your hands to feel whether it's working. However you do it, think of energy building up inside you, and tension flowing away. Rest quietly now.

7. *Alternate nostril breathing*

Hatha – the word Hatha – is thought to mean Sun-Moon. There is a connection between this idea and the idea of left and right.

Breathing with the left and right nostrils in turn is a very ancient part of Hatha Yoga. It can be extremely restful, and has been known to produce some surprising effects connected with deep relaxation.

Let me show you: I place the index and middle fingers of my right hand on my forehead. Now I place my right thumb on my right nostril, my fourth finger on my left nostril and my little finger next to the third. So I can now close whichever nostril I please. I can perform all kinds of breathing sequences:

– in through the left and out through the right;
– in through the right and out through the left;

– in and out through the left;
– in and out through the right.

Try it for yourselves.

Sit in a cross-legged position: sit up straight. Place your right hand as I did: I'll show you again.

Clear your nasal passages: have a good old sniff.

Now close your eyes: start to breathe very slowly and very gently.

Now start to breathe in through your left nostril and out through the right.

You'll have to go *very* gently. Don't make a sound: just feel the cool air passing in, and the warm air passing out.

Rest your elbow: no need to have it up at an angle, getting tired.

Rest your hand now.

Hindus wouldn't use their left hands, for reasons of ritual, but we can.

Put your left hand in position, and breathe the opposite way.

Now use either hand, and use one nostril at a time for both breaths.

Some of you may feel slightly light-headed, or even dizzy. This is quite common: and I would ask you not to do too much nostril breathing on your own. This powerful effect is one more way in which Yoga breathing is strongly connected with relaxation, mind control and deep meditation.

8. *Sustained vocal breathing*

When you breathe out, you let the air pass through your mouth, or through your nose, and that's all. You can do it quickly or slowly, and you can listen to the hiss, or the swish, of the breath as it passes through. This simple process, as we've seen, can be the prelude to relaxation, the innocent background of meditation, or the key to control in postures.

But today we're going to be different. Listen: I'm going to take a full breath and, as I breathe out, I'm going to let the breath set my vocal chords buzzing and then escape through my nose.

(Breathe in, and then emit a long, sustained HUMMMM-MMMMMMMMM . . . .)

Now you try!
Voices: Any special note? – Won't it sound awful, I mean: we're all different! – I can't sing a note!
Teacher: Just try! I'll do it with you: and you just mind your own business and don't worry about anybody else!
Breathe in . . . 6. 7. 8.
Now! Hum! MMMMMMMMMMMM . . . . (Die away).
This has most useful effects on the sound spaces in your head – a kind of internal massage! Try it again, and really let your head vibrate with the sound!
Breathe in . . . . 6. 7. 8.
Now: HUM! louder! Let the whole room vibrate with 20 (?10, ?30), humming sounds . . . .
Die away now, to nothing . . . .
We'll come back to this in the chapter on meditation.

9. *Explosive breathing*

Stand up: alert, erect, and still.
Fill with air.
When I say 'go', let it all out in a rush . . . . GO!
Rotten! (Several voices, laughter etc.)
Try doing it this way: as you breathe out, flop forward – like this. (Do so.)
Now you try. Three things to do:
 (a) Stand well and breathe in full.
 (b) Pause for a moment.
 (c) Flop forward and squeeze all the air out in a rush.
So: Stand well – breathe in.
Pause – and – FLOP!
Much better! Now try something else.
Instead of letting the air rush out and flopping down, shout: AH! or ARGHH! – mouth wide open. You'll have to forget completely about me, and the class. I'll do it first, then I'll do it with you.
Listen to me first:
Breathe in . . . 6. 7. 8.
Pause.
SHOUT! (Do so.)
(Class usually taken aback by this: laughter, chatter.)

Right – the moment you've been waiting for! A chance to shout your worries away! No swearing please!
Breathe in . . . 6. 7. 8.
Pause, and – SHOUT . . .!
Good! Once more!
Breathe in . . . 6. 7. 8.
Pause, and . . . (let the class shout on their own).
All right, cough, splutter and sniff for a moment!

10. *Special movements of the abdomen, to improve breathing control*

(a) *Squeezing the diaphragm:* Jane finds this hard, but she is getting better at it, and says it has made her breathing more positive – more satisfying. Watch what she does: I'll help by pointing things out as we go along.
She stands, legs well apart, hands pressing on front thighs. She takes a full breath; releases it; squeezes it out, and then watch: with her lungs empty, she

- lifts her chest,
- expands her ribs,
- and draws her tummy muscles up high, so that there is a little hollow each side, where the rib cage begins,
- lastly she lets everything go, and breathes in, pauses, and rests.

Watch again (repeat – rest). (Put a fist into the hollow – to prove it's there.)
When you become familiar with the movement, you can try doing the 'lift' two and three times, before finally resting.
Now it's your turn! Try it on your own, and try to use a fist, to see whether you've got anything like a hollow!!

(b) *Moving the stomach muscles:* Some people, usually slim, athletic people, find they can do this. Jane can't really do it, but she can show you how to start. Maybe some of you do it better! If so, please come along to the front and show the rest!

When you've done the 'Diaphragm Squeeze' and can do it quite well, try using mental concentration and physical pressure, to force the stomach muscles well forward so that they look like a great, strong band of muscle, standing out from the rest of the abdomen.

If that seems possible to you, and you get used to it, try moving that band of muscle to one side, and then to the other. It all helps to strengthen all the important breathing muscles in the abdominal region.

11. *A simple Yoga breathing sequence*

As years, centuries have passed, a sequence for breathing has been developed. It's a sequence which you can apply to abdominal breathing, chest breathing, shoulder breathing, by themselves, or to all three, strung together in full Yoga breath.

The sequence tells you how long to take over breathing in, how long to hold your breath and how long to take over breathing out. After each cycle you can either go straight away to another cycle, or do some gentle breathing for a change.

The sequence is based on the numbers 1, 4 and 2. For instance, you could treat these numbers as seconds: i.e. take one second to breathe in – hold for four seconds – breathe out for two seconds. But I defy anyone to do it like that and really enjoy it, or get anything useful from it! I suggest we think in terms of double quantities: 2, 8, 4. Watch Jane (in Corpse).

She's going to breathe in (she will choose her own style) for 2, hold for 8 and breathe out for 4. I'll count. (Do so. Jane breathes.)

Now you try!
Breathe in 1. 2.
Hold 2. 3. 4. 5. 6. 7. 8.
Release 2. 3. 4.
It's *still* too fast, isn't it?
Try again – we'll go for 3, 12 and 6! (Do so.)
Now rest . . . .
Anyone game for 4, 16 and 8? (A total of 28 seconds.)
I won't count out loud, just count my taps for yourselves. (Do so.)
Now! What about 5, 20 and 10? (A total of 35 seconds.) If you can't manage it, just do what you can . . . . *(Tap.)*
Go on trying this for five or six cycles, with rests in between. While you are doing it think not only about the details of your

new breathing exercise, but about some of the other things that go with breathing:

1. Complete relaxation: feet, legs, thighs and hips; fingers, hands, arms and shoulders; neck, head, eyes, face, lips.
2. Peace of mind: thoughts gently resting on the sequence of your breath.

Breathing is the constant companion of good Yoga: to be used, on its own, as a way of 'changing gear', of slipping easily into a different emotional mood, or as a necessary background for relaxation: gently rising and falling as you slip further and further into a 'holiday of the soul'.

In the next two chapters we shall see how postures and movements, and later, meditation, play essential parts in Yoga. In both, breathing – I mean the best breathing you can achieve – is vital.

9: Teaching Postures

Introductory note

Postures tend to loom large in the outsider's impression of Yoga. We all know what someone will say if we tell them we teach Yoga, and we wait with the standard reply: 'Oh, it's much more than that. . . .' Maybe we should be really honest, and say: 'Oh, it's much *less* than that . . . .'

Certainly postures make an excellent framework around which you can build an interesting Yoga evening, or a good series of Yoga evenings. But we must, sooner or later, ask: 'Are postures, routines, movements and sequences the goal to which I am aiming in my Yoga teaching? Or are they the means whereby I help my pupils to achieve relaxation, concentration, contemplation and meditation?'

Bear in mind too that everyone in the room – teacher, demonstrator, or pupil – has limitations, and you cannot, and must not, teach postures as a challenge, even less as a series of progressive hurdles.

What confuses the issue even more is that many in the class have probably only come for the postures, because that is what they think Yoga is all about! Many of them will not be aware of their strengths and weaknesses until they find a posture which is quite beyond them.

Before attempting to suggest how ten or so postures might be taught, we must list a number of vital points about postures that teachers must bear in mind when they are planning and teaching them:

1. Postures are only one of the classical eight paths of Yoga.
2. Their immediate aim is the development of physical balance and control of the body.

3. Performing postures well also involves concentration and the need to be free from nervous and emotional tension.
4. Postures, in turn, contribute to and develop concentration, and relaxation of the nerves and emotions.
5. Many postures stimulate the heart, massage internal organs, or provide healthy exercise and deep rest for limbs and joints.
6. Of the 84 postures suggested by the Indian Yoga Master, Patanjali, there will be many that beginners can attempt, and learn to do well, but the selection will differ from person to person.
7. It is better to perform an easy posture very well than to strive without success with a difficult one.
8. To be quite correct, one should approach postures with a clear conscience. Failing this, being absorbed in postures will often bring a moral resolution to attend closely to one's personal life (the first two paths of Yoga).
9. Postures are intended to be natural, and should be treated as such.
10. Many pupils, though probably not all, will want to combine breathing, relaxation, postures and meditation, and this is a most worthwhile aim. But the foundation of this final combination must be good performance in each part.

Teaching the Cobra (see Figure 4)

Teacher: I want to introduce you to the Cobra posture. Gather round the platform. This posture is called the Cobra because it's rather like a real cobra raising its head. Let's watch Jane perform the whole posture.

She starts in the prone position, lying on her tummy, arms by her sides, resting her cheek on the floor, wholly relaxed, gently breathing.

Now she's ready to start. She sets her mind to the posture. Her body becomes alert: head, arms, legs, spine. Breathing is normal, but controlled.

She slowly brings her hands up in line with her shoulders, palms down, fingers level with the line of her shoulders. She has her chin on the floor and looks straight ahead: she braces her legs, and her spine becomes strong and supple.

Now for the movement. Her head rises, eyes lifted, looking

high. It curls back on her shoulders. Her shoulders lift up and back, her spine curves up and back. She lets her chest expand, and she lets her arms take some of the weight.

Now the movement is complete. She is looking immediately above her, eyes looking even further back: the spine is curved, from shoulders to hips, and her arms are gently angled, giving support to the posture.

The returning movement repeats the first movement, but in reverse. The spine returns to the mat progressively, from the abdomen upwards. The arms give less and less support: the chest relaxes. The head is last to return, and eyes still look high. When the chin touches the floor her body gradually resumes its position of complete relaxation.

Voices: I could never curve my back like that! – Can you press with your hands, to help you? – Must you keep your hips on the floor?

Teacher: Very few of you will manage it like Jane, at least to begin with, though you *may* get a surprise; it's the curve in the back that is the secret and the real aim of the posture: any kind of curve is better than none!

Don't press with your hands more than you can help. You certainly mustn't straighten your arms: it ruins your back position and can do harm to your shoulders, and your wrists.

The Cobra is a spine movement, not a body movement: your lower body, including your hips, and your tummy almost as far as your navel, should stay on the floor.

Jane: I like to do it very slowly so that I have time to think about everything that's happening outside and inside: many different pressures and stretches. It feels very stimulating in the extreme position.

Voice: How can you breathe when you're right up in that stretched position?

Jane: I breathe gently and slowly. I have to: it's the only way I can do the posture properly. I have to breathe right, think right and feel right. Sometimes it's ages before I can bring myself to begin the movement, and I always lie quite still for a long time afterwards. Shall I do it again?

Teacher: Yes, and I'll point out some vital details:

1. The movement is continuous: head and eyes leading the way.

2. The spine curves, from the top: the shoulders move gracefully back and the chest expands.
3. The head drops back: the flow of the body line is very pleasing to watch.
4. The return movement, too, is supple and sinuous.
5. At the end, a gentle but complete relaxation.

Now it's your turn: go to your mats.

Lie prone: . . . . . relax.

Hands in position: look at your fingers.

Follow my instructions. Breathe gently all the time.

Look up, brace your body.

Raise your head: look high. Your shoulders follow. Don't push on your hands: feel your back muscles doing the work. Let your shoulders slip back and your chest expand, making the fullness of the curve: feel your arms begin to unbend: don't straighten them. Can you see the ceiling? Any further?

Back you come, from the hips upwards. Feel the floor coming up to meet you, your arms closing on themselves, your head slowly, smoothly travelling back. Breathe gently all the time. Chin touches the floor. Turn onto your cheek: let softness ease into every joint, relax completely . . . .

Voices: You wouldn't believe it could be so demanding! I couldn't do another one!

Jane: It was like that when I first started: but I've learned to do it carefully, thoughtfully – keeping my energy carefully rationed.

Teacher: It amounts to what I often say to you: *relax into your postures*. Postures are ways to perfection: the perfection is far away, and not within your understanding yet.

Teaching the Bow posture (see Figure 5)

The Bow posture is a good one to try when you're just beginning Yoga. There's so much to it that it will keep you busy for quite a long time in a session: it looks quite spectacular, and feels quite unlike any other experience. And it has very powerful good effects on your general posture, the internal organs, the blood supply, and the muscle-tone of your shoulders, your thighs and your legs. In one of the variations you can even massage yourself!

I'm going to ask Jane to perform each of the three standard

versions, and the massage variation. Stay on your mats, because you can only learn this one by doing it yourselves. When you've seen Jane, we'll give her a rest, and then ask her to do the Bow again, with you. It's one of many postures which have the advantage that you can watch the teacher or the demonstrator while you're doing it!

Jane starts prone and relaxed.

She takes up the ready position: body alert and ready for action.

Breathing at the moment is normal but controlled.

1. Reaching back with her left hand, she raises her left foot, 'captures it' with her left hand, and holds it, by the ankle, comfortably.
2. She then does the same with her right hand and foot.
3. She pushes her feet back and up, using the muscles in her legs and thighs: the effect is that the feet exert a pull on her hands, and these in turn, on her arms and shoulders. Her spine curves up, she looks high and throws her head back.
4. She relaxes the posture: lowering her head, letting her knees bend again, and allowing her body to return to the floor, but maintaining the hand grip on her feet (or better, her ankles).
5. Carefully, she lets her feet go free, rests her arms, and brings her feet slowly back to the floor.

Notice: I haven't said anything about knees, or whether the feet should be together or apart. This is because there are two variations where these are concerned. Jane will perform what I call 'the Narrow Bow'. Notice as she goes through the routine: the knees touch, all the time, and the feet do as well. The effect is a much more emphatic drawing back of the shoulders.

The other variation is 'the wide bow': the knees are as wide as possible, and the feet are really wide apart. This allows a strong, sudden pull up, with the effect that the body rocks backwards with the power of the thrust, and then forward, with a little help from the arms: in other words, the body is rocking to and fro, and, in the process, massaging the lower abdomen, and the organs within.

Now it's your turn. On your tummies, please, and completely relaxed.

We'll do the standard version first. If this is too much for you, do your best and then rest. Many of you will want to try the other two versions, and the rocking motion.

Good: now listen to me, but watch Jane! She is facing sideways to you so that you can see the details.

So: lift one foot; capture it; hold it gently captive. (Regular breathing.)

Lift the other foot; capture it; hold it gently captive.

Now: push your feet back and up, and, surprise, surprise, your shoulders start to lift!

Throw your heads back: look high.

Now, gently bend your knees, lower your feet, lower your head, disengage your hands, rest your arms, and let your feet slowly down *together*.

When your feet touch the floor, flop completely.

Voices: Phew! Gosh!

Teacher: Yes – I know! It's the first time and you've tried too hard! Many of you bent your arms: just follow the instructions – I didn't say anything about pulling with your arms! Now try it in your own time: if you feel strong enough, first with your feet and knees close together, and then with them wide apart: try to rock your body to and fro . . . .

Teaching the Shoulder Stand (see cover photograph)

Teacher: The Shoulder Stand: one of the classic Yoga postures. It will take us many weeks to learn it, and while we are learning it, we shall be so taken up with remembering what to do, that we may not notice any immediate effects. In fact, as with so many postures, it's only when you can do them without thinking that they really begin to help you.

I think we would be well advised to divide this posture into (1) getting there, (2) staying there, and (3) getting back. Just for the present, we will concentrate on the posture, and not bother too much about what happens before and after.

Jane will assume the correct Shoulder Stand position: she tells me that she can hold this position for quite a long time, so I'll keep her up there, and point out the main elements of the posture.

1. The whole body is inverted – upside down. Its weight is taken on the shoulders: hence its name.
2. There are three main body lines:
   (a) absolutely perpendicular, from the midpoint of the feet, down through the body, to the shoulders.
   (b) horizontal: from the elbows to the back of the head.
   (c) 45 degrees: the forearms, supporting the back.
3. Notice that the chin is pushed well into the chest. In this position the blood circulation, the internal organs, and the muscles receive benefit from being completely reversed.

Now we'll let Jane rest, whilst we try to manage our first attempt.

We must go carefully.

Lie in the Corpse posture; rest; breathe normally.

Become alert, from top to toe. You can't see, so you must listen, imagine and perform: that's good Yoga anyway!

Bend your knees and slide your feet in towards you.

Bring your knees up over you; use your tummy muscles to raise your hips; go up as far as you can without strain.

Now prop yourself up on your hands and finally straighten your legs. Pause for a moment.

Now, very carefully, bend your knees again; put one hand back on the floor; now the other as well.

Use your hands to steady yourself; let your hips down; feel your feet touch the floor; slide them gently away from you, and . . . *rest* . . . .

Sit up and watch again.

Now I'll ask Jane to show you what most of you did: it's sometimes known as the half-Shoulder Stand. (Jane assumes the posture.) Notice that her back is only half-way up; her legs are way over her head, and her hands are almost on her hips. Now watch as she improves her posture by simple steps: moving her hands, her back and her legs. (Jane rests again.)

Try your own movement again: when you get up there, try moving one hand, then the other, and straightening your body up by degrees. Don't worry this week about getting there gracefully: think about that final position, and don't expect miracles!

Remember to come down with your knees bent, and under control! No falling or bumping allowed!

Teaching the Plough (see Figure 6)

The Plough posture is a movement just as much as a position. From the moment you begin, every detail of movement in every joint and muscle is part of the posture. To make things rather demanding for the beginner, it has an uncanny simplicity. There are so many things about the posture, that, like the Shoulder Stand, we must take it in stages. You've spent the last two or three weeks trying lifting movements, and backward tumbles: now for the real thing.

Watch Jane. She lies in the Corpse, breathing gently. I leave you to notice what you can and tell me afterwards. Now: she begins to move, or rather her legs do. In fact, it's only her legs, and her back, that move; up, up and over; coming to rest behind her head; toes touching the floor, and legs naturally straight. She pauses for a moment, and begins to return – again a very simple movement (or so it seems): back and legs curling back the way they came, until they come to rest, and Jane relaxes.

But it's easier said than done! While she is resting tell me what you saw.

Voices: When she started her tummy went tight. – Her hands moved as she went over. – At the end, when she was nearly over, it was the hip joint that let her legs down.

Teacher: What about when she came back?

Voices: Her back didn't move until her feet were off the ground. – Her hands moved forward a bit as she came down. – Her tummy was tight at the end, then it relaxed.

Let's ask Jane!

Jane: I like this one very much: I listen to myself as I go along – different muscles coming into action. Sometimes, if I lose concentration, I come down too quickly, and my head lifts right up off the ground.

Teacher: What I want you to remember is the extraordinary movement of the feet – a pure half-circle. Aim for that: a slow continuous movement, both ways. Any lack of control anywhere will cause wobbles and break the flow. Prepare for each change of muscle-power like runners do in a relay: avoiding dropped stitches!

Jane can rest now, while you try the movement by yourselves. Don't try to reach the floor. Getting some of the way there properly, this time, is much more important than actually arriving!

Teaching the Pose of Tranquillity (see Figure 7)

The Pose of Tranquillity is a beautiful, restful posture. Once again, it is deceptive. There is a moment of balance which you must find! It's rather like the Plough, but more advanced (I think). Jane will make the movement for us: it starts like the Plough, but the legs stay up, almost parallel with the floor. When she feels well balanced and secure, she moves her arms, and arranges her hands as supports for her legs. This arm movement alters the balance considerably, so it must be done with gentle concentration, but no strain. The return is the reverse of the outward movement. Arms return to the floor, and the body curls back . . . and rests.

Breathe gently as you go. You may find that your breathing rocks your body to and fro: keep it gentle, or you will rock yourself back with a bump!

Generally speaking, breathing in opens the body and breathing out helps it to close. Use this rule if you want to synchronise breathing with movement.

At other times you can observe a different rule: don't breathe while you are moving – don't move while you are breathing.

But that is a major item in Yoga, and we will look at it another time. Now it's your turn to try the Pose of Tranquillity.

Teaching the Backstretch (see Figure 8)

This time we're going to turn everything round: I want you to try to do the Backstretch, then I'll let you see what Jane makes of it!

Kneel back on your heels, with your feet flat. Later we can try it with our toes tucked underneath.

Now find a comfortable place to put your hands, and lean back on them: look at me.

Now let your head gradually fall back.

As it goes, lift your chest and arch your back.

Lastly, tuck your tummy in, and look right behind you. Pause a moment. Take the strain out of the posture . . . . Now release your tummy, let your chest recede, relax your shoulders and lastly, *slowly*, raise your head.

You can combine a breathing sequence with this one, if you like: breathe in as you go back, and breathe out as you come forward again.

How did you get on?

Voices: Not too bad. Couldn't do much with my stomach: couldn't seem to move it, in or out! – I got a pain in my jaw – I felt I wanted to cough – Doesn't half stretch your wrists! – It's my feet that finished me off!

Teacher: You've just about covered everything there! Let's apply all those points to Jane.

Jane has taken up the posture: notice just a few of the many points about this position:

1. Her legs are really folded: you can only just see her feet.
2. Her tummy is quite flat.
3. Her chest is expanded and her shoulders drawn back.
4. Her head is thrown right back, and she is looking directly behind her – her vision is in line with the floor.
5. Her arms are vertical: her hands are immediately below her shoulders.
6. The only breathing she can do while she is waiting is with her chest.

Now it's your turn again: but this time, turn to face away from me. We'll do it all together: I'll count four times, five for each stage: five to start breathing, five to stretch back and finish breathing in, five to ease forward, and five to breathe out. When you stretch back you must try to see me, and I want to see everybody's eyes! Ready?

Breathe in 2. 3. 4. 5. Stretch 2. 3. 4. 5. Come on, I can't see everybody! Good. Relax 2. 3. 4. 5. Breathe out 2. 3. 4. 5. Rest.

Teaching the Camel (see Figure 9)

The Camel is like the Backstretch except that you kneel up, not down. Now you'll have to watch Jane because it matters quite a lot how you do it.

She starts as if she were going to do a Backstretch, but after a pause to collect her thoughts, she slips her hands in under her, grasping her heels.

She keeps on looking straight ahead, and thrusts her hips forward until her thighs are vertical: can you see how straight they are! In fact, if she were just learning the posture, she might release one hand, and inspect her thigh line. (But it's hard putting it back again!) When she's satisfied, she arches her back, draws her shoulders back and looks directly behind her. Notice: vertical arms again!

The value of course is the powerful movement of the hips: you'll notice this when you do it (and afterwards as well!) A lot depends on whether you have long arms too. Some people have to rest their fingertips where Jane is using the whole hand; or else they can tuck their toes underneath: this raises the heels two or three inches.

There is another way of arriving at this position, but we'll deal with that another time.

Jane's going to come down now: notice that she lifts her head first, and then pauses until she's ready to lower her hips; then she rests completely.

Voices: Do you have to be up straight? – I couldn't look that far back! – What about breathing?

Teacher: You will be up straight to begin with. If you know that it's beyond you, don't do it. Doing it badly is very tiring, looks awful, and is a waste of time. How far you look back depends on how supple you are: that will improve in time. Meanwhile, go as far back as your spine will let you, but relax into it – don't push into it. Breathing: either gentle all through, or breathe out when you throw your head back and in again when you come forward.

Now: into the ready position. Jane's resting, so think about it, and follow my directions.

First of all, is it toes out or toes under? You must try one or the other first, you can choose your preference later!

Now slip your hands in and get a good grip on your heels. Keep looking straight ahead.

Now: push your hips up, forward and away . . . feel your thighs coming up straight. Look at other people's for a moment: there's every angle in the book – and some very straight ones. Now: keep looking forward.

Ready? Now: let your head tilt back . . . pause . . . breathe gently – rib breaths of course – that's all you can do!
Coming down: *lift your head first*, so that you can see where you're going, then pause. Think what you're going to do: and slowly, powerfully, lower your hips again. Slip your hands out from under you, and I suggest you go forward into the all fours position, or sit down, so that you can remedy any stiffness in your feet.

Teaching Twists (see Figures 10 and 11)

Teacher: Twisting your body, carefully and thoughtfully, is one of the most completely effective ways of manipulating and massaging your internal organs. And of course there are quite obvious healthy pulls and stretches on the limbs and joints.

There are so many twisting movements that we could do a different one every week for a term without repeating ourselves!

We'll confine ourselves to the spine twist in the seated posture. There are two stages. Let's start with the simple version. Don't bother about how to get there: just concentrate on what the finished article looks like:

1. The legs are turned to your left, the body faces you, and the head is turned to your right.
2. The limbs are placed in such a way that they lend support and natural energy to the posture:
   (a) Jane's left leg rests: her right leg crosses it, creating the beginning of the twisting motion.
   (b) Jane's right arm follows her right leg, and grasps her right ankle, giving a twist to the shoulders. Her left arm is vital. It does two things: it gives added twist to the body, from the shoulders, and it supports the spine, giving the whole body an alert, upright, pleasing appearance.
3. Between the hips and the shoulders, the body undergoes a continuous twisting process, both outwardly and inwardly.
4. Head and eyes follow the trend of the twist, providing a feeling of completeness.

Clearly Jane finds this easy, and so she tackles a further stage. This time she tucks her left lower leg underneath her.

Her right knee is higher and her right arm exerts considerably more pressure: there is, incidentally, valuable careful stretching of the thighs. The body twist is more marked, and the left hand support more necessary.

The body must be erect, vertical. The head and eyes follow the line of the twist, as before.

This upright, tidy posture may be very difficult. It depends very much on the proportionate lengths of your legs, your body and your arms. There are many other, more advanced versions. Try it.

Sit on your mats, like Jane: legs out in front of you, body erect, arms beside you, hands close in, to give you good vertical support.

Lift your right foot, and place it on your mat, outside your left knee, flat. I expect you can feel a bit of twisting happening already, in the pelvic area.

Bring your right hand over and grasp your right ankle: bring it right up and over the knee.

Now stop and check your back. *Don't let it flop over.*

Put your left hand on the mat, behind you, but right up close to you; feel your body twisting right round as you go; let your shoulders rotate; feel the twist having its fullest effect at your waist.

Lastly, swing your head round and look right round to your left, at natural eye level.

Breathing gently and regularly this time.

Check your spine again . . . .

Come back the way you went, only in reverse . . . .

For the other twist movement, begin by folding your left leg in against your right: your left foot right up tight into your left thigh. This has the effect of pushing your left knee way off to the left. Bring your right foot over, as before: it's a much bigger movement this time! But do it properly just the same. Your right knee will be up in front of you, so slip your right arm over and across it, and use your right elbow, pushing against your right thigh, as a lever, pushing you round to the left. Keep checking your spine-line; move your left hand right behind you, look hard left, and stay still. Breathe deeply two or three times. Come back the way you went, only in reverse . . . and rest.

Teaching the Cat posture (see Figures 12 and 13)

You could spend a week just learning the all-fours position. Try it now – good: stay exactly as you are. Check the following items, one by one:

(i) Left hand exactly under left shoulder.
(ii) Right hand exactly under right shoulder.
(iii) Left knee under left hip.
(iv) Right knee under right hip.
(v) Back natural: not too high, not too low.
(vi) Look naturally at the floor: about three feet ahead.
(vii) Breathe gently.

– and rest! Sit and watch.

Now we can look at the Cat. It's called a posture, but really it's two postures which alternate, and the movements between them are very important. You've got to concentrate on several movements at once, and try to create one single flowing action.

Let's look at the two extreme positions.

First the high position. Jane's arms and legs are unchanged: they are still in their all-fours positions. But her back is arched: the highest point is the point where the shoulder-blades begin; and her head is low, her face way down – looking between her arms.

Now the low position. The hands and knees are hardly any different: it's just that the effect of the movement is a slight change of direction. But notice the back and the head: the back has really collapsed – its lowest point is at the waist. And look at the head: it's raised to a point half-way to vertical: the eyes (at least Jane's eyes) can see the ceiling.

Now for the movement. You must get from one position to the other in one transition: head and body moving together, but in opposite directions! You'll probably find you want to bend your arms, or sit back towards your heels! Don't!

But you can see how it involves the progressive interaction of the vertebrae and the head. Several groups of muscles are involved and you must just patiently wait until you discover where they are, and how to use them.

Jane: I couldn't do it at all at first: now I've learned what it feels like to do it properly and I recall that feeling to mind when I'm doing it.

Voices : It looks simple enough. It doesn't seem to need special strength or suppleness.
Jane : No: it's just getting yourself to move in the right place, far enough, at the right time!

Teaching the Locust (see Figure 14)

The Locust is more deceptive than most postures: nothing much seems to happen. The only bits that move are the legs. But there's all the strength in your body involved in that movement. You can use one leg at a time, or both together. Let's look at the two-leg version first, and then work up to it!

Jane lies on her tummy, relaxed and breathing deeply. When she's ready she braces her body carefully, slips her hands underneath her, folded tightly into fists. Then she slowly raises her legs, from the hips, pauses, lowers them, and finally replaces her hands by her sides and relaxes again.

Can you see how it works and how it's donc?
Voices : It must be thigh muscles, and back muscles. – It seems to tighten the buttocks too – that's useful! – I would have thought her head would have risen.
Teacher : The secret is in the hands. With two fists right underneath you, you can push down on to the floor, just where it matters, and the result is the lifting of the legs: you'll be surprised!
Well: try it! . . . . Now, rest!
Voices : My head popped up: I couldn't stop it! – I got my legs quite high, I think.
Teacher : But many of you got your feet high by committing the commonest mistake in the Locust: bent legs! There is a certain natural angle at the knee, but you must do the lifting, not at the knee, but right up in the hip.

Keep in the back of your mind the extreme form, attained by experts in India, who raise their stomachs as well – leaving their hands all alone on the floor!

Teaching the Child (see Figure 15)

After a group of postures, or at the end of a Yoga session, people often like to perform the Child posture, just once.

Let Jane have the platform to herself. Watch in gentle silence as she eases herself down into this childlike, embryo of a posture, all folded up neatly. Three major folds in the body: the knees, the hips and the shoulders, with lesser folds at the neck and elbows. Breathe gently and meditate on the three great lines of the body: back, thighs and calves, and the deep rest of the arms.

You can achieve this feeling of finality, the feeling that this posture can only come at the end of a session, if you ease yourself into it very slowly.

Start by kneeling back on your heels, and curling down, from the crown of your head, bone by bone. When you arrive in the position, imagine that you are sinking even further . . . into a calm rest which sums up all that you have done in your relaxation, your breathing and your postures.

Concluding Note

The space we have been able to devote to each posture in this chapter has been very limited. It would be as well if we recalled the aim of the chapter, and of the book as a whole, which is to shed some light on the problems and pleasures of teaching Yoga. If the postures appear to have been treated with less than the appropriate depth, this is in the interests of devoting space to all the necessary topics in the book, and also because postures in their own right are treated at considerable length in the standard text books (see *Further Reading*).

10: Teaching Meditation

Introductory Note

In any Yoga session, the teacher must have in mind that whether he is aware of it, or intends it, or not, he is doing two things:

(a) subjecting his class to the procedures of Yoga, and thereby procuring for his pupils, as far as they are able to attain them, the benefits of Yoga.

(b) training his class in the various ways in which they may perform Yoga by themselves, without his presence to guide them.

This division of the Yoga teaching process is particularly true of meditation. He is leading meditations with the class, so that a meditation actually takes place during the session; he is also teaching his class how to meditate by themselves. He is showing them how to use meditation procedures in his absence.

In this chapter we shall speak, as usual in the class situation, of teaching pupils how to meditate, and then, in the second part of the chapter, speak about leading actual meditations in the session. The two are in many ways very different, and must clearly be seen to be so.

Teaching Yoga meditation methods

Teacher : Each week, when you relax, I ask you to think quietly but carefully and clearly, about the way your body is gradually becoming soft, rested and still. That quiet thinking is a kind of meditation. Meditation is just thinking about a single, simple subject: at least, that's how it starts.

It's the same with breathing: when you think about your breathing you may have begun to let your mind be aware of your breathing, without thinking too precisely about what is happening. That's the beginning of meditation, too. As we go on progressively in Yoga, I shall teach you how to meditate through your postures.

You can also meditate with your eyes, your ears, even your nose and your mouth. But one thing at a time!

Remember that *you* have a vital part to play in learning Yoga. The art of Yoga is a very private and personal affair: for many people a Yoga class is a contradiction: 'How can you have an intimate, personal experience in public?', they say! But whatever you think, it is true that you should try to find time between sessions to do Yoga on your own. I am really only here to suggest ways of doing Yoga, give you help in exploring them, and then leave you to go on and try them on your own.

As you go along, remember that behind all our varied activities there lies an ancient road to perfection, and meditation lies nearer the end than the beginning. In fact, at the beginning, there are two conditions that we ought to bear in mind before we take so much as our first step onto a Yoga mat.

The ancient paths of Yoga, in order, are these:

1. Self-control (*Yama*): Do not be violent. Tell the truth. Be honest. Control your desires. Be generous.
2. Goodness towards others (*Niyama*): Be single-minded. Don't be greedy. Live an ordered life. Be aware of your own strength and weakness. Be ready to recognise the presence of mystery in life.
3. Postures (*Asanas*).
4. Breathing (*Pranayama*).
5. Withdrawing the senses: detachment (*Pratyahara*).
6. Concentration: attention without tension (*Dharana*).
7. Meditation (*Dhyana*).
8. Bliss: union with the Divine (*Samadhi*).

You'll notice that meditation is well down the list: number 7 to be exact! But it is natural and congenial to western culture to progress in any of the first seven stages, as far as you are able, without regard necessarily for their order of sequence, always keeping in mind that the last step is an experience which very few have achieved.

On the other hand, stages 5 and 6 are, apparently, considerably advanced, even though they appear to come before meditation. This is why you should think of these eight parts as being not so much a series of hurdles or challenges, as degrees of depth to which you may or may not penetrate at any point in your 'Life in Yoga'. Now we'd better start!

Meditation through relaxation

Lie in the Corpse posture: go through the usual relaxation process . . . now you are lying in deep repose, with your breathing regular and shallow.

Now let your mind begin to share this relaxed feeling: let your thoughts be concerned with your feelings of relaxation, as if from a distance, and become aware of a very compelling idea that is classic in Yoga: that your mind and your body are not as closely connected as you may have thought. It is possible, perhaps quite easy, to see your body in quite a detached way. You can say to yourself: 'My body is very relaxed: I am watching my body relax.'

Can you understand that this is rather like the 'detachment' I mentioned, as the fifth path of Yoga?

Meditation through breathing

What we have learned about meditation through relaxation is also true of breathing.

Try the Corpse posture again, or you may prefer to sit cross-legged, or to arrange your hands and fingers for alternate nostril breathing.

But instead of thinking hard about your breathing, think 'easily' about it: sit and 'watch yourself' breathing. You can talk mentally to yourself about it: 'I am taking breath into my body: my lungs are nearly full . . . now my body is becoming empty of air again . . . .'

Here again, you are involved in gentle breath control (*Pranayama*), detached observation of your own sensations

(*Pratyahara*), and are beginning to experience something rather like the 'attention without tension' (*Dharana*) which is the step nearest to meditation proper (*Dhyana*).

With breathing there is often an added 'dimension', the involvement of emotions. It 'feels good' to take a deep breath, and sigh it all away: it's a release of nervous and emotional tension, and this in turn has its effect on the first two paths of Yoga. It works in two ways:

(a) the moment you realise that you can stand back and actually watch your emotions advancing and receding, you gain confidence over the matter of self-control (*Yama*), and your relationships with other people (*Niyama*);

(b) at the same time, growth in Yama and Niyama helps you to have a much more deeply satisfying meditation.

The paths of Yoga have become a circle!

Meditation through postures

Teacher : I know what you're going to say: 'Postures are hard to do well! It takes all your attention. You can't meditate in the Cobra!'

But you can! You ought to try.

And we shall!

There are two postures, apart from the Corpse, where meditation comes naturally: the pose of Tranquillity and the Child. In these postures, you can stop and think what you are doing: let the thought become a vague awareness, and finally 'float on a mood of stillness'; it's Pratyahara, Dharana and Dhyana again!

And there's another development here too: you begin to notice that if you can observe your body and its sensation objectively, watch your emotions ebb and flow, and finally, watch your thoughts becoming progressively more simple, then something fundamental has begun to happen. You become aware that there is something inside you which is doing all this observing, watching, being detached and being aware. What is this 'something' which is not physical, emotional, not bound up with sensations and nervous experience, and distinct from thought? Could it be the real 'You', describe it how you like?

And so to:

Absolute meditation

This is the fruit of what has gone before, though there are some who by the nature of their temperament can by-pass some of the steps.

To be able to recall the experience of meditation at will, in moments of stress: this is an aim dear to the hearts of convinced Yogis. It is possible only by the regular exploration of the relaxation techniques, breathing, postures, not to mention the moral and ethical precepts of the first two paths.

Leading a meditation

INTRODUCTORY NOTES TO TEACHERS

1. Two alternatives present themselves:
   (a) to set aside a time for meditation proper;
   (b) to present the whole session within the context of meditation.

Normally it proves most effective to establish a good 'meditative' atmosphere throughout, but to specify one part of the session as exclusively meditation. But even so, the meditation will be more effective if it is prepared for with insight, and followed up with sympathy. This in turn raises a number of other points:

2. *When should meditation come in a session?*
The middle and the end are favourite 'slots', but much will depend on circumstances. Certainly, it should be prefaced by relaxation and breathing, and should be followed by a natural break or discussion.

3. *How much direction should be given?*
People's needs differ very much. It should be made clear that any meditation is only an idea presented for trial by interested members. Those in the class who have developed their own method should be encouraged to 'do their own thing'. But there should be a period of silence: the length tailored to suit the circumstances. Two minutes is perhaps the minimum, but

is enough for a simple exercise on a cold evening with a large class of varied abilities. With a small advanced group, up to twenty minutes is not excessive: but only if the room is quiet and warm. The natural effects of meditation on circulation and body temperature are factors to bear in mind: the exercise is better too short than too long.

Finally: anyone who leads a meditation must be modest, but a leader nevertheless. The class are in his hands: he is privileged to have, for a few minutes, direct access to their consciousness, and he must, to quote a remarkably apt phrase from a different context, 'beware of treading on their dreams'.

Meditation on a candle flame (see Figure 16)

Needed: A candle in a sturdy holder, set safely with the flame twenty-four inches from the floor; a room which can be darkened; a group of no more than fifteen to twenty people, seated crosslegged as near the candle as possible. The leader should sit or stand outside the circle. The candle is not yet lit and the room lights are still on.

Teacher: Is everyone comfortable?

Voices: I feel a bit out of it. – Come in here next to me: we can open the circle. – I don't feel very relaxed. – Shall I take my glasses off? – I can see people across the circle: will I have to stare at them?

Teacher: You can come in as close as you like: it doesn't matter if you're touching the next person. Don't worry about not feeling relaxed: I'll soon change all that! Glasses on or off – doesn't matter. You won't see anybody else, once we start.

Now: I'll light the candle, give it a few moments to burn full, and then we'll have the lights out. While we're waiting I'll say something about candle meditation. It's one of the most popular ways of meditating, and you can do it with a group. Group meditations can be very memorable experiences, and we can discuss this afterwards. Whilst we're meditating, just follow my lead and see what happens. If you get uncomfortable, you can move about a little bit. Cough if you need to. Generally feel at ease . . . . Good: now we'll have the lights out . . . .

Sit easily. Breathe deeply but gently. Think about the room in darkness, about the group gathered in one space . . . about the circle within the group . . . about the candle . . . and begin looking gently at its flame. Let your eyes rest on the flame: on its shape, its colour, the way it moves, its gentle brightness. Try not to look so much as just see it – let your eyes rest on it: a kind of contemplation. If you want to blink, do so, but try to do without blinking . . . when your eyes grow tired, persist a little bit longer, and then, quite lazily, let your eyes close . . . . Now let your mind's eye rest on what you imagine you can see: I hope you may have an image of the flame: quite small, glowing in a variety of colours; perhaps you have a radiant haze around the image. It may grow brighter and then gradually begin to fade. Watch it fading, see it disappear, and let your mind's eye rest on the space where the image used to be . . . .

In the two minutes' silence now, go on looking at your image, or the darkness where it was, and if your mind wanders, think about your breathing, and then return to the image . . . .

. . . The meditation will end very soon now: begin to prepare for a more alert frame of mind. Breathe deeply three or four times . . . . I'm going to switch one light on (do so). Watch how I deal with the candle: I blow it out from below. Never blow the candle out from above: the heat is greater than you think! If you try this at home, have the candle about fifteen inches from you, and at eye level.

Now: how did you get on . . . ?

Meditation on colours and stars and water

Lie in the Corpse posture . . . go through your relaxation and breathing routines . . . settle to regular deep breathing. As you breathe, try one of the following meditations: they will help you to find the 'attention without tension' which is only just a little short of meditation (or Dhyana).

Colours: When you breathe in, call to mind a colour. With each breath you take in, the colour becomes more vivid; when you release your breath the colour fades a little. So, to begin with, concentrate on deep in-breaths, and let your breath out very slowly. In the silence, let the breaths, in and out, be equal. As the meditation closes, breathe the colour out and away.

Stars: When you breathe in, a number of stars appear in a dark sky. As you go on breathing the number of stars increases; their brightness depends on your powerful in-breath. In the silence, contemplate the stars, see patterns: groups of four or five, clusters of three, a haze of many smaller stars. As the meditation concludes, breathe the stars out and away.

Water: When you breathe in, you see water in a stream: clear and bright. You see the stream's bed: sandy and marked here and there with stones. When you breathe out, the water becomes turbulent and cloudy. In the silence keep the water clear. When the meditation concludes, let the water fade from view . . . .

Meditation on sensations

Note: it is, oddly enough, the experience of many teachers that using actual objects of sensation, perhaps carefully prepared and even at some expense, is not appreciated by pupils as much as the imagination of such objects. Try real objects if you like, but remember that classes are quite happy to do without!

Teacher: Lie, sit or kneel, in any comfortable position. Breathe gently and deeply. Close your eyes . . . .

Choose one of the following articles: an orange, an irregularly-shaped stone, a flower, a roll of paper. Imagine that you have it in your hand . . . .

Feel it against your finger tips, the palm of your hand . . . .

Contemplate its weight, its size and texture . . . .

Explore its shape . . . .

Press it for a moment, in your mind, against your lips, your eyes, your nose, your ears . . . .

Explore the sensations that come through your senses . . . .

In the silence, do three things in your imagination:

1. Go through the sensation routine for the last time.
2. Put the object down, and recollect the sensations.

3. Take the object again and check the sensations against your memory of them.

When the meditation ends, breathe deeply and arouse within yourself a more alert mood.

Meditation on Om

Note: this meditation is appropriate for a group who have a common outlook on the philosophical assumptions of Yoga, notably the idea of a Universal *Self*, who is sometimes known by the title *Om*.
Teacher: Let's conclude this last session of the present season by coming together in a circle . . . .
Sit in Lotus, Half-Lotus, or your own chosen cross-legged posture . . . .
Begin to breathe in the classic Yoga sequence: one, four, two . . . .
Let your eyes half-close; let your vision rest just a little in front of you; observe the emptiness in the middle of the circle . . . .
Let your mind dwell on the emptiness . . . .
Now we will begin to breathe together:
in – 2. 3. 4.
hold – 2. 3. 4. 5. 6. 7. 8. 9. 10. 11. 12.
release – 2. 3. 4. 5. 6. 7. 8.
(Three times)
Breathe gently now, don't sustain the breath: begin to control the out-breath . . . .
As you breathe out, let your voice begin to sound the name of the Self Universal: OM . . . .
Breathe in 2. 3. 4. 5. 6. 7. 8.
Breathe out . . . OOMMMMMM . . . .
Go on doing this at your own speed . . . Let OM become a continuous sound echoing round the group . . . .
Be immersed in the sound . . . feel yourself at the centre of the sound . . . .
Imagine yourself sinking downward into the depths of the sound, and into the depths of the Self . . . .
Let the sound go on, and on, and on . . . .
Now the sound begins to fade . . . .

It gradually fades . . . and . . . stops . . . .
Silence: recall the sound . . . recall the Self . . . .
Be the Self.
THOU ART THAT . . . .

Concluding Note: There is little more to be said, but there will be many who report new sensations, stimulating experiences, frightening feelings, the urge to shout. One may be in tears or feel the wish to cry; many will report intense emotion: love, hate, bliss, or, often, absolutely nothing. Some will claim that they have not heard the content of the meditation, or were not aware that there had been one.

Everyone will be surprised at the passage of time, will have felt a sense of abstraction from their immediate surroundings: a kind of floating.

All will observe a slowing of the pulse, a lowering of body temperature.

Some will ask about Samadhi. It is very difficult to answer these many questions: they are personal questions, to be personally answered. Those who are convinced that they have experienced Dhyana should perhaps see a personal teacher to proceed any further.

But, whatever the case, it is an occasion for joy, increased friendship in the group, and the greater fulfilment of personal life for everyone, not least the teacher, who will find great happiness in the warmth of Yoga life in his class.

11: Special Kinds of Teaching

Certain kinds of students need special kinds of teaching. This chapter professes to do no more than offer suggestions of a general nature. The best source of ideas and expertise is experience, but we have to start somewhere.

Classes for children (not as part of the school day)

Children like Yoga, or rather, they like many aspects of Yoga. Which aspects they like will depend not only upon age but upon temperament, and unfortunately for us it is quite impossible to predict what will be beneficial, or enjoyable, for any one child. This is the reason why children's classes are very difficult to run well: the needs, physical, emotional and mental, at any one moment are so diverse that the teacher cannot hope to cater for them all. And the classes tend to cover a wide range of ages, abilities and backgrounds: this is natural and right. We have in mind classes organised on a voluntary basis, perhaps in the early evening, or on a Saturday. What tends to happen is that young people (mostly girls) of 12–14 form the foundation of these classes: they have an enviable suppleness and just the beginning of a feel for relaxation and mind control. A little later they tend to be joined by younger sisters and brothers: this opens the flood gates and children as young as 3 years may appear. These latter may bring their mothers, either as 'minders', spectators, or participants. So this is the problem. Let us list our class members again. Let us imagine:

- 6 experienced girls of 13 years,
- 8 boys and girls of 7–11 with little experience,
- 6 young children of 3–7 with no experience,
- 4 mothers.

It is essential to have a good concerted beginning (some good standing full breaths, or perhaps the four Mudras) and then, inevitably, there must be subdividing of the group, and we have reached the point where having several teachers is the only answer. The six experienced girls will need advanced postures (they are surprisingly adept and will need an expert teacher). The eight with little experience can stay together and make steady progress. The very young children will need specialised treatment: patience with those whose concentration is nil, and who really prefer to run round and round the room! They like seeing postures as animal shapes, and like repeated movements. The mothers will, if you make the right tactful approach, help the tinies. At the end everyone should come together again for a quiet five minutes, perhaps with a candle (safety measures please!), or a large mandala. If facilities allow, they should be encouraged to change. Many of them positively delight in taking a shower, and this is even better. Be very particular about the safety side. Expect to be 'handed' parcels of youngsters by parents who are unashamedly pleased to be free of them for an hour or so, but hand them back safely afterwards, and be prepared, now and then, to look after the odd waif whose parents have been delayed!

Classes for children in school time

These tend to come in three kinds, and are very much on the increase.

1. *Relaxation, breathing and postures as part of Physical Education:* Without doubt there is a need for Yoga as a leaven to Physical Education. We need to learn how to be still, be calm, and be controlled. Ideally there should be a Yoga 'slot' in every PE lesson, for children up to thirteen. This, of course, presupposes that PE teachers have had some training. Where this is not so, courses should be held for existing PE teachers, either residential weekends, or a group of regular weekly meetings.

2. Young people of 13–16 might profitably be given a Yoga option during PE time, and an opportunity to learn about Yoga as part of Religious Studies. Team games and organised PE are not popular with many teenagers, and Yoga is one of

several possible alternatives. But once again, either in PE or RE, we must *not* allow tuition from persons without training or experience.

3. Sixth formers, and for that matter college and university students, need adult-type Yoga; but remember that they often tend to be intense, sometimes expecting early results, sometimes rigid in their likes and dislikes of various aspects of the subject.

But in many ways, a well run students' class can be one of the most rewarding experiences in Yoga. These young men and women who spend so much of their time in high-powered mental activity – observing, making deductions, expressing themselves, making emotional attachments – show quite disarming pleasure in being able 'just to relax' for an hour. They often hang on the teacher's words, and show a gratifying sincerity and earnestness in their postures, their breathing and their meditation. They begin to get interested in the esoteric and mystical aspects, and this needs a note of warning. Open discussion about drink, smoking and drugs is probably the best way of defusing a potential explosive tendency in the introvert and the temptation to flirt with the socially off-beat in the extrovert.

Classes for elderly people

These classes come in two sorts:

(a) Classes for elderly people who want to keep themselves active. This category would also include elderly people in ordinary classes.

(b) Classes for elderly people with various common handicaps: stiff backs, failing sight or hearing, or simply the need to 'take things easy'.

(a) Many old folk are 'game': ready for a few carefully chosen activities, and very much in need of training in the art of complete relaxation.

For them a progressive programme is best. Start with training in sitting properly in an upright chair and waiting patiently for the tension to ebb away from the legs, the arms and the neck. Rest then and talk about this experience.

Go on to breathing training, still seated on chairs: abdominal, diaphragmatic and clavicular, as far as they are able.

Again – more discussion.

Close eyes, and think quietly about some favourite holiday spot in the sun: perceive the emotional quality of serenity and mentally 'store it away' for use in the unexpected crisis, or the moments of loneliness.

Lastly, some simple finger, hand and arm movements, and some gentle head 'flops'.

It helps enormously to have an elderly demonstrator, just to show them how an older person would go through these various procedures: they might find it hard to 'pick it up' from a young teacher.

In succeeding meetings they can proceed to a limited number of standing movements, and eventually to some supine positions, though they will need, and probably want, support under the small of the back, and some kind of neck pillow.

(b) Old people with handicaps need individual help. But they should also have some group activity. For many of them the class is a precious time for meeting other people and they should do at least a little together, and certainly have time for discussion, or just gossip!

Yoga has much in common with physiotherapy, and even those who are confined to an invalid chair can do something: breathing, arm movements, and gentle neck and head twists. If they give all their attention to this they will find it a very pleasant change from their normal habits of life, and this in itself will make the class worthwhile.

Older people also seem to have a sympathy with the ethical limbs of Yoga, and can see that a serenity inside is necessary to a tolerant and generous attitude to other people.

Anyone with a real interest in Yoga for handicapped people should try to win the confidence of the local health-visitors, physiotherapists and doctors. There is a great deal that Yoga can contribute to medicine and a Yoga teacher on the staff of every general hospital is an idea that deserves more than a passing thought.

Yoga for seriously handicapped persons

Yoga is particularly suited to deaf persons. A teacher working with deaf people will quickly become accustomed to using gestures to indicate breathing, movements, and even mental concentration. Deaf people's eyes are very often endowed with special sensitivity: use this to draw attention to quite small details of perfected postures, and help students by manually correcting mistakes.

Blind people can be taught Yoga too. Here, of course, the burden of the teaching must be borne by word of mouth: a great test of oral dexterity, and a challenge to the most extensive vocabulary! Certain sequences of words will soon become part of their pattern of work, and you must abide by them. This may mean that you have to compile, and keep adding to, a 'blind people's Yoga phrase book'. Test your expertise on a normal class, by asking them to close their eyes, and then estimate the degree to which they follow your instructions to the letter. Here's an example:

Stand straight: feet together and arms by your sides.
Gradually feel yourself standing better, standing taller.
Brace your legs together; point your fingers downwards.
Head up; look straight ahead (yes: they will know what you mean!)
When I say 'Now' let everything go loose again .
Now!
Start again: brace your legs, point your fingers.
Go on doing it, and breathe in as you go along, while I count to 8: 1 . . . . 8.
When I say 'Now' let everything go loose and let all your breath out in a rush.
Now!

Your 'phrase-book' is likely to be pretty thick – but either you will begin to learn the phrases by heart, or you can keep it by you for reference.

Here again, give individual help by manual correction, but explain this to them first: learn their names, and 'call each one up' as you approach, so that they know you are going to touch them.

Mentally, nervously or emotionally handicapped persons often benefit greatly from Yoga, but it is doubtful whether they can, or should, be taught either in large groups, or individually. A small group of four or five is probably best, and postures 'for the fun of it' is often the most acceptable activity. Meditation, or even simple relaxation, sometimes frightens them – they feel lonely, and are afraid to be face to face with themselves. Some of them will find Yoga immediately helpful, and, paradoxically, may be frightened by the possibility that they may actually be getting better!

Certainly the need to be fit, the need to be able to breathe freely and think clearly has led many a compulsive alcoholic, chain-smoker, or potential drug addict to put the thing aside because 'it stops me doing Yoga properly'!

Speech defects, blushing, agoraphobia: these and many other ailments have been conquered by the need to *concentrate* on Yoga. A problem once forgotten often ebbs away unnoticed and you wonder why it ever caused you so much anguish.

Meditation groups

A group, as opposed to a class, has no regular leader or teacher.

Something intangible happens when the teacher gathers the class into a circle at the end of a session and takes part with them in a final meditation. The atmosphere engendered by the group is in some way deeper than the feelings of its individual members. This is especially so if the object of the attention is a candle, flowers, or something similar, placed in the centre.

This particularly appeals to some students, and teachers sometimes get requests to arrange meditation groups.

A group of beginners who want to meditate should be guided by the teacher, and left to do their group work, preferably at the end of a session, for about fifteen or twenty minutes, finishing a little before time so that the teacher can discuss their experience, and answer questions. They will probably have success most readily if they begin with breathing, take their cue for contemplation from one of the group (probably in rotation), and end with a mantra together and several moments' quietness. The teacher should beware of 'over-reactions' to meditation experience, which can be emotionally quite dramatic.

As a group becomes experienced it will tend to shed less enthusiastic members, and gather new members. This can present problems. One of the things that make a meditation group successful is the close relationship of its members. A new member can be an embarrassment, and must realise that he may not 'fit' – through nobody's fault.

It would be as well if the teacher gently insisted on being an occasional guest, to prevent anyone becoming over-enthusiastic, overdoing the joss-sticks, or introducing doubtful avant-garde practices.

A good group could be left alone entirely. In fact, there is much to be said for allowing an advanced group to meet as it pleases. An urban Yoga centre should, ideally, have a Yoga Teachers' Association attached to it. This group would contribute towards the cost of running the centre, and in return might have weekly access to a room or rooms, without supervision. Once a month they should meet in formal session, perhaps with a visiting speaker, and to pursue any Association business.

Such a group, or any group of advanced students, would benefit from a residential weekend, as described in Chapter 5. Occasions like this provide many opportunities for unsupervised Yoga, whether physical or mental, and it is fascinating to see groups forming quite spontaneously at weekend sessions, which may very well stay together afterwards, for regular weekly or monthly meetings.

Private pupils

Sooner or later teachers are asked: 'Do you give private lessons?'. We referred to this in brief in an earlier chapter; now we must look into it rather more carefully.

Teachers must ask themselves, at an early stage: 'Am I a private teacher type?'

What is a 'private teacher type'? Surely someone who feels no apprehension at being face to face with a complete stranger in a one-to-one situation. Someone who feels competent enough to win the confidence of a pupil who for some reason wants private rather than public coaching. Someone whose home circumstances are such that Yoga teaching there poses no problems: these could either be connected with the noise and rough and tumble of busy family life, or by contrast, connected with living alone, or in limited accommodation. Remember that private coaching is a telling drain on physical, mental and nervous energy: can you survive? Finally, you must search your conscience and make sure that your motives are above question, and your request for a fee (or not, as the case may be) based on sound reasoning.

What is the 'private student' type? Someone who has some reason to prefer private to public coaching. A shy person? A lonely person needing someone to confide in? An 'unusual' person, perhaps with problems greater or more complex than you can deal with? Perhaps even a person with a dubious motive wishing to place the teacher in a compromising situation (yes, it does happen).

What form do private sessions take? Any form. The first meeting should begin with small talk, and the exchanging of routine information: name, address, age (roughly), experience, reason for wanting private lessons, history of any inhibiting ailments, fees. The teacher should then give an account of what Yoga involves and suggest a few minutes' practical work. Depending on the reaction of the pupil, some simple relaxation, breathing or postures might follow. Then another short discussion: 'Do you want to continue?' 'Yes'. 'Well, I suggest that you try a sequence of activities' – and write them down. A hand-out with pin-men would help at this point. Finally, 'Would you like another session – say, in a month's time?' Allow them to choose whether to make an appointment on the spot, or contact you again later. If they write or ring to cancel, or just don't come for their next appointment, don't pursue the matter: it is probably their way of saying 'I've changed my mind.'

Future sessions will follow the needs of the pupil or the wisdom of the teacher, and perhaps lead to the pupil joining a public class. Private coaching might also be a way of training a teacher in the absence of a local group-course.

Remember that one-and-a-half hours is the best length for

a private session, and that one pupil an evening is enough. This means that thirty such pupils, coming once a month, means one every night. Need we say more?

If you want to have private pupils, ensure that you are properly qualified and that your qualifications are visible in the room, and announced in the national Yoga magazines.

Special lectures and demonstrations

When a teacher becomes established he will begin to receive invitations to speak to groups of people who are not Yoga students and are not interested in the subject other than as one of a number of subjects which their organisers think are topical, and will provide an interesting evening (or afternoon). This does not, of course, mean that there may not be Yoga students in the group; maybe it would be unwise to assume so, just as it would be unwise to assume that they know nothing. They are likely to have seen television programmes and glanced at magazines. Such groups are ladies' circles, women's institutes, The Professional and Business Women's Association, young wives, slimmers' clubs, and the like.

The experience of giving a talk to a group like this can be stimulating and very rewarding, or devastating! So much depends upon preparation beforehand, and the right 'management' of the event. Here are some do's and don'ts, mostly the fruit of bitter experience!

1. Establish clearly, in writing, in advance: the date, the time (i.e. (a) when the meeting starts, (b) when the talk begins, (c) when your talk ends, (d) what happens after that) and the venue. Be quite exact – which room, how big it is, and what shape it is, and what the seating will be.
2. Establish the position about fees and expenses, and having negotiated them, stick to them.
3. Find out what the precise programme is to be, e.g.:
   – talk (by yourself), and questions;
   – talk and demonstration, by yourself, and questions;
   – talk, with a demonstrator or team of demonstrators, with the demonstrator(s) joining in the discussion;
   – talk with slides (NB plugs, sockets, 5 amp, 13 amp, screen, projector, flex extension, etc.!);

– talk, with some of the audience joining in some simple practical work;
– and there are many more permutations!

4. If you do not have a car, mention it – it's nothing to be ashamed of! Get yourself fetched and carried!
5. Remember that you are talking about Yoga to the uninitiated, many of whom will have some odd ideas. Proceed with care, so that you commend your subject, and, who knows, swell the ranks of the local classes!
6. Don't expect hushed attention! Groups differ a great deal, and you may have to introduce yourself and establish your own atmosphere of interest and respect.
7. Don't expect ideal conditions. Many unforeseeable problems can arise.
   The thing to do is to take these things as 'part of a day's work'. Be seen to be the unflappable and genial guest: it will do much to commend the subject!

Giving a full scale demonstration to, say, an audience of college PE or dance students who are 'keen to have a go', can be most rewarding. For some of the audience it will be perhaps their first chance to meet a real Yogi (or Yogini) and you may be quite overwhelmed by the pedestal you feel you are standing on. Go along with this to a certain extent, otherwise you will shatter all kinds of genuine respect they will have for you and for Yoga.

The best kind of full demonstration is a miniature version of a normal Yoga session. Don't rehearse your team, but be rather more careful than usual about 'talking through' each part of the programme, explaining what is happening, why, and what the benefits are. Afterwards, invite the audience to get into conversation with the demonstrators: it may produce more honest and direct questions and answers than if you had asked for questions against the silent background of a sea of faces on both sides of the 'footlights'. Seat the audience in a great horseshoe, round the demonstrators, who sit in a circle, facing the centre, but not so near each other, or the first row of the audience, as to cause embarrassment!

Look after your demonstrators – fix the footbound with lifts, and the driver with travelling expenses. If it's likely that you will get regular engagements, discuss the possibility of uniform leotards or shirts and slacks.

As the subject continues to gather momentum, the mass media will make increasing demands upon successful teachers. Talking and demonstrating on television is a very special technique; but this is really a subject for a specialised article rather than a useful part of a general teaching manual.

We have a great paradox in teaching Yoga. We are employed to display to others what is, to us, a very personal and intimate art. It is the dilemma which faces educational drama too: why should children have to express their own free dramatic expression to the gaping eyes of an uninitiated audience? But there is one difference, and it lies in the fond and heartfelt hope that those who hear a good talk, see a good demonstration, or are fortunate enough to be members of a good class, will have a yearning for Yoga awakened in themselves and will see the teacher as the generous betrayer of his own secret happiness, and will 'go and do likewise'.

12: Yoga, Religion and Life

Sooner or later the teacher of Yoga must come to terms with the relationship between Yoga, religion and life. He must thoroughly understand it in his own mind, otherwise he cannot claim to be conversant with what he is teaching; he must live sincerely by his understanding of that relationship, otherwise he will be continually in a turmoil of unrest, or will enjoy the false security of self-deception or hypocrisy; and he must fearlessly convey his understanding of that relationship to his pupils, in such a way that they respect his integrity, and are encouraged to grow into their own understanding of the relationship between the three basic ingredients of the most personal and intimate aspects of the subject.

We have already established that this book is not a textbook in Yoga, and it would not be appropriate to embark on an enquiry into the origins and nature of Yoga, the nature of religion, and the aims and commitments of personal life; but it is essential for anyone wishing to study the origins, history and varieties of the Yoga ideal to make use of the best modern scholarship. It is with this thought in mind that I recommend the following:

1. Mircea Eliade. *Yoga : Immortality and Freedom.* Routledge & Kegan Paul, 1958.
2. Ninian Smart. *The Yogi and the Devotee.* Allen & Unwin, 1968.
3. S. G. F. Brandon (ed.). *A Dictionary of Comparative Religion.* Weidenfeld and Nicolson, 1970.

What follows, in this chapter, is an attempt to put Yoga, religion and life, into a perspective that can be grasped without any great mental effort, and conveyed to a class of beginners. For, make no mistake, like children, absolute beginners in Yoga can be guaranteed to ask those very questions which are hardest to answer!

What is Yoga?

Yoga is different things to different people. It has very special meanings for the Hindu ascetic, the Buddhist monk, and the devout Jain, in India. It has rather different meanings for the Vedantist, and the student of the writings of Ramakrishna. It even has different meanings in the writings of Patanjali, in the Upanishads, and in the Bhagavadgita.

But what is Yoga for Mr Brown, and his class of beginners in Bluebell Secondary School, Middleditch, on a cold, wet evening in November? It is, surely, at the very least, the following things:

– it is a discipline (Yoga: a yoke, a harness, a rule);

– it has an immeasurable claim to our attention, based upon many centuries of experience in the East;

– it has been well tried for a century or more in the West;

– it boasts the testimony and support of many great figures, from all walks of life, and thousands of happy people in classes all over Britain. One recent estimate suggested 300,000 as the number of those currently studying Yoga;

– it teaches that man is composed of: a body, a mind, a personality – a notion well supported by the generality of scholars concerned with the nature of human existence;

– it teaches that the body needs careful attention, not only by way of growth and activity, but by way of rest and relaxation;

– the mind likewise needs training in observation, deduction and decision-making, but also in the putting aside of objects of attention, the passive contemplation of ideas, and the willingness to defer decision-making, to let the mind lie dormant;

– the personality – what makes us persons rather than complex machines – needs to be encouraged to express itself, not only actively, through the mind and body, as so often, but also passively: to observe itself, recognise itself for what it is, and to be content. In the words of many a happy pupil during discussion after meditation: 'It's nice to have ten minutes absolutely to yourself.'

– for some there is an added, rare moment, when, as it seems afterwards, a little time has passed, and 'you simply have not been aware of its passing'. This could be described as a moment of 'liberation', and may be the ultimate aim of some pupils.

– but for most pupils, Yoga's purpose is to put right the stress and strain of daily life where the personality is absorbed in frantic, and often tiresome, mental activity, and exhausting physical effort. Yoga puts things right: restores the balance, sets you on your feet again, gives you a centre of gravity.

– but it doesn't happen without effort, and in Yoga the effort is carefully structured: the pupil is presented with sequences, tailor-made, and undertakes the yoke, in order to achieve personal balance and integration.

What is religion?

Religion is different things to different people – the religion a person follows is usually an accident of birth. It does not help to imagine fondly that all religions are really the same. Some people may think so, but it will not be true unless everybody thinks so! However religions, political ideologies, and personal aims, tend to be recognisable:

(a) There is usually (but not always) a founder, prophet or messenger;

(b) There are stories, myths, and facts of history;

(c) There is usually a God (or gods) but not always. Sometimes there are gods who are not directly involved in religion;

(d) There are beliefs, and these are usually formulated into doctrines or creeds, which members are expected to accept;

(e) There are ways of worshipping: sacrifices, rituals, prayers, involving temples, shrines, priests and offerings. Here again, it is not always the case: is quiet meditation a kind of worship? If a man believes that he can be united with his god in meditation, can he believe that his god should be worshipped?

(f) There are sacred, or semi-sacred books. Sometimes the books themselves constitute objects of worship;

(g) There are ways of approaching god, and ways in which he approaches man. Either way, man seeks god – seeks to be saved from the world – seeks rescue, or salvation. Again, for some, liberation from the world does not necessarily involve approach towards, or union with god;

(h) Life is affected by religion, so religions have ethical expression – ways of living which are in keeping with the faith;

(i) There is some kind of belief in the form life will take after death: from nothingness, through 'heaven – hell – purgatory' beliefs, to reincarnation, and to permanent liberation – a kind of Nirvana;

(j) There is usually some kind of belief about the origin of the universe, the power underlying it, and the nature of life: animal, vegetable and human;

(k) Lastly, religions and ideologies have external forms and symbols: art, architecture, dress and life-style: diet, feast days and fast days, and ways of celebrating birth, growing up, marriage and death.

We have said something briefly about Yoga, and something briefly about religion. Perhaps readers have noticed that although each has, hopefully, been a complete and faithful representation, there is no necessary overlap. A Yogi need not be religious, and a religious person need not be a Yogi. But, and this is the burden of the following section, life is there to be lived, and a proper Yogi and a religious person may very well lead similar lives, or at least, lives that are similar in many respects.

What is life?

Life is the span of existence between birth and death. Anything before birth or after death is a matter of speculation, faith, doctrine, intuition, or (who knows) experience.

It is lived in the context of the family circle, the making of a home and a career, and the satisfaction of seeing a new generation rise to adulthood.

The way we live, pass each day, each week; the way we

relate to our parents, or friends, our children; and reactions to crises, to moments of decision and moments of truth: all these things will be the result, or perhaps the expression, of a complex array of attitudes in our minds (quite apart from the effect of the state of our health at the time). These attitudes may be religious, cultural, political, emotional or instinctive, and we shall very rarely be aware of the cause-and-effect process which is going on.

The process of living presents a complexity which defies definition and refuses to be sorted into compartments. But there are three comments about the process of living which are very relevant to our purpose:

1. Unhappily, the majority of people allow days to pass, marking the passage of time by the arrival of a pay-packet, the next instalment of a television serial, the demands of the domestic occasion, be it birth, marriage or death.

2. Many deeply religious people are influenced more than they are aware by the suppositions and presumptions of their faith, mistaking outward symbols – rites, habits, attitudes – for personal and heart-felt insights.

3. There is a third approach to life which avoids these two extremes. It comprises an honest self-knowledge, an understanding care for others, and a serious appreciation of the deeper issues of life. The way of life which this person leads will depend on the circumstances of his birth and family life, and upon many other things, but whatever that way of life is, it has the added ingredient of healthy thoughtfulness and restful industry. To this third approach the practice of Yoga can be of immense significance: enhancing self-knowledge, aiding physical and mental health, and illuminating the world of existence. Yoga adds a new dimension of depth to personal life, regardless of creed, culture or commitment.

The Yoga way of life

The preceding paragraphs may seem superficial: it is easy enough to make statements of a general nature, not as easy to be more explicit. The remainder of this chapter presents a 'menu of Yoga living' from which any dish will provide its own kind of nourishment. It is a Yoga teacher's privilege, and duty, to present this menu to his class, or, more correctly, a selection of menus. But he must make it clear that the choice of dishes is absolutely free, and that no dish is obligatory. For those who want a 'structured diet' he must present reasoned arguments for a particular selection.

We will imagine that we are meeting a variety of Yoga pupils, whose backgrounds are very different, and who derive from their sessions very different benefits.

1. Let us, to put things in perspective, begin with two extremes:

(a) John Brown has had three years of progressive Yoga: he spends one hour every evening in his room 'doing his Yoga'. He is twenty-five, unmarried, and teaching in a local school. He does postures, breathing and meditation. He burns joss-sticks, has a corner of his room fitted as a shrine with a candle, an image of the Buddha, and posters of Krishna and Guru Maharaj-ji. He is a vegetarian, and spends large sums on health foods. He is saving for the time when he can afford to visit Rishikesh, and now and then he wonders whether he may stay in India.

(b) Mrs Betty Smith is thirty-four, and has a growing family. She manages to get to Yoga class because her husband looks after the children. She does an hour and a half's Yoga on Wednesdays, at the class, and that's all she can manage, apart from living her busy life a little more steadily, taking crises as they come, and doing some deep breathing to help her to get to sleep. She says she's less snappy with the children, more able to cheer her overworked husband, and even manages to be nice to an aged in-law who makes demands and offers little thanks!

2. Then there is Mary, twenty-five, a secretary, who came in the first instance because she had 'seen it on television'. She enjoys the relaxation, or rather, enjoys the gentle stretches and deep breathing that make up for all the time she spends at work, taking shorthand, bending over a typewriter, and dealing with many things she doesn't understand, and doesn't really care about. After her routines, at class, and her breathing, she enjoys just 'lying flat out' and 'dying' (Savasana). She says she's too 'flutter-brained' to meditate properly yet, but

likes to be still and contemplate garden scenes. She is less tense than she was a year ago, is eating less, and improving her figure no end. Her friends tell her that there is a calmness in her face and a clearness in her eyes, which she is sure is due to generally feeling more at ease with people, and less self-conscious. She doesn't much care for philosophy, and never was very religious, but is a permanent Yoga student, in her own way, at least for the present.

3. Jean is just married. She has given up her job (in a department store), has means to begin a family. The family is Catholic on both sides. She is not very supple, and frankly, doesn't enjoy postures, though she recognises similarities between Yoga relaxation and what she has read about natural childbirth. What she does find fascinating is the relationship between her own religion and Yoga philosophy. She was brought up to believe in the majesty of God, the mystery of the Trinity, the loving humanity of Jesus, and the power of the Holy Spirit in every human soul. The centrality of the Scriptures, the gift of Grace through the Sacraments, the promise of Life Eternal, and the Communion of Saints, are the bread and butter of her religious life. Now she is studying the Eight Limbs of Yoga and exploring the various Yoga Schools, notably Bhakti Yoga, expressed in the Bhagavad Gita, with its emphasis on devotion to the God of Love, and Karma Yoga, also in the Gita, clearly setting out spiritual progress in the context of the good life, and service to others. She is not carried away with any idea that the two systems are the same, or even similar. What has happened is that she is thinking about her own religious life more clearly: making her own faith a matter of personal affirmation rather than acquiescence in accepted dogma.

4. Father Stephen and a group of Anglican monks at a local Community have found aspects of Yoga a very real help with their spiritual exercises and their daily lives. Good posture, proper breathing, and mind training has helped in meditation, and this in turn has given them better daily health and a real dynamic sense of purpose in their duties inside and outside the Community House.

5. Mrs Green brought her twelve-year-old daughter to a children's class, almost as a last hope. Young Sandy was the family failure. Quite brainy, but very moody, and poor soul, quite un-coordinated. 'I've tried her with dancing, swimming, horse riding – she's so clumsy, you've no idea: how much is it per lesson?' Sandy *was* clumsy – the sort who begins to stride left hand and left foot together! What mother didn't realise, and this was Sandy's salvation, was that Yoga makes no demands, none at all, at first. Then as you gain confidence, you can allow yourself to face growing challenges, and they are all your own choice. Sandy tried sitting cross-legged; tried sitting cross-legged properly; tried the four Mudras, then the Cobra, the Child and the Swan: and managed them. Each week she went home delighted, only to find that her younger sister could 'do them' straight away. 'All right', she said, 'you come along next time: then we'll see!' The two sisters became avid pupils.

6. Mr and Mrs Smith came as senior citizens: 'Oh, we didn't realise it was like this.' But they agreed to sit on upright chairs and found that there are a great many things you can do with your hands, your feet and your head. They learned about breathing. They were interested in starting a little group of their own, and the group had some very exciting sessions: sitting round a candle, taking it in turn to lead a meditation. They had a break and sampled home-made pastries and savoury sauces. They grew herbs, and brought flowers for their meeting room. They took a delight in a little bit of mysticism, mixed with astrology, and even experimented with group vibrations: holding hands, and revolving to face magnetic North. The local Yoga adviser went to see them now and then, and offered them suggestions on ways of extending the variety of their activities.

7. Peter and Eileen came together. They were College of Education students. Peter was studying drama for his main course, with Religious Education as his second string. He found Yoga interesting in very many ways, particularly as he was intending to teach about all the world's religions, and Yoga provided a practical way of being quietly contemplative, without being committed to a particular faith. His dramatic

enthusiasm also found an outlet, for he saw many of the postures as ways of expressing personality, just as a great deal of Christian ceremony is dramatic expression of a heart-felt commitment. Eileen was studying Physical Education, with music, art and dance-drama as other interests. Yoga was not taught at College, and she found another dimension to the self-awareness of the body in postures, relaxation and breathing. She also found Indian music and art a delightful contrast to their mainstream European counterparts. Both of them meant to try to get Yoga onto the time-tables of their schools.

8. Joan, recently divorced, had been on heavy courses of sedatives. There was a history of religious obsession in her life too: she was altogether a confused, unhappy person. What she found a real blessing in Yoga was the peace and quiet of the relaxation, and the fascination of the Brahman/Atman idea. She was intrigued by the distinction between Dhyana and Bakhti, and between communion with the divine, and liberation from self. She became something of a mixture of a Christian agnostic, and Theravada Buddhist, and a Hindu Vedantist. All these new interests drew her out of her old self and helped her to become a new person.

Of course, all the persons described here are fictitious, but they represent a fair proportion of those who come to Yoga, and find in it opportunities to discover new depths in religious experience, should they choose to, and fundamental influences on their lives, if only they will permit them.

The subject is so large, that there is no one who cannot find pleasure, challenge and benefit in it. It is educationally respectable, psychologically sound, and physically rewarding.

Above all, Yoga is a life-style which has something to offer to the bodies, minds and hearts of twentieth century society.

Further Reading

1. M. Eliade: *Yoga: Immortality and Freedom*, Routledge & Kegan Paul (1958)
2. B. K. S. Iyengar: *Light on Yoga*, Allen & Unwin (1968)
3. Swami Vishnudevananda: *The Complete Illustrated Book of Yoga*, Bell (1961)
4. T. Barnard: *Hatha Yoga*, Rider (1968)
5. Rachel Carr: *Yoga for all ages*, Collins (1973)
6. H. Day: *Yoga Illustrated Dictionary*, Kaye and Ward (1971)
7. M. Oki: *Practical Yoga*, Japan Publications (1973)
8. Prof. C. Raven: *Anatomical Atlas*, Pitman Medical (1970)
9. R. D. Lockhart: *Living Anatomy*, Faber (1963)
10. R. Hutchinson: *Yoga Health and Beauty*, Arthur Barker (1970)
11. A. Van Lysebeth: *Yoga Self-taught*, Allen & Unwin (1971)
12. P. Gervis: *Naked they Pray*, Cassell (1956)
13. P. Brunton: *A Search in Secret India*, Rider (1970)
14. N. Smart: *The Yogi and the Devotee*, Allen & Unwin (1968)
15. Patanjali: *Yoga Aphorisms (How to Know God)*, Mentor (1970)
16. *Bhagavad-Gita*, Mentor (1968)
17. Hittleman: *Guide to Yoga Meditation*, Bantam (1969)
18. Dechanet: *Christian Yoga*, Search Press (1965)
19. Ramakrishna Monks: *Meditation*, Ramakrishna Vedanta Centre (1973)
20. Hittleman: *Yoga 28 day Exercise Plan*, Hamlyn (1971)
21. Swami Sarasvati: *Yoga for Vital Beauty*, Harrap (1973)
22. Pandit Shiv Sharma: *Yoga and Sex*, Harrap (1973)
23. Volin and Phelan: *Growing up with Yoga*, Pelham (1969)
24. Volin and Phelan: *Yoga for Women*, Arrow (1970)
25. R. C. Zaehner: *Drugs, Mysticism and Makebelieve*, Collins (1972)

Detailed list of contents